Me 262
Hitler's Jet Plane

Me 262
Hitler's Jet Plane

Mano Ziegler

Translated from the German
by Geoffrey Brooks

Grub Street | London

This hardback edition of *Me 262: Hitler's Jet Plane* first published in 2023 by
Grub Street
4 Rainham Close
London
SW11 6SS

Me 262: Hitler's Jet Plane is a translation of *Turbinenjäger Me 262*, which was first
published by Motorbuch Verlag, Stuttgart, in 1978.

Copyright © by Motorbuch Verlag, Postfach 103743, 70032 Stuttgart
English language translation © Lionel Leventhal Limited, 2004

British Library Cataloguing in Publication Data

Ziegler, Mano
Hitler's jet plane : the ME262 story
Germany. Luftwaffe – History – World War, 1939–1945
Messerschmitt 262 (Jet fighter planes) - History 3. World War, 1939–1945 –
Aerial operations, German
I Title
623.7'464'0943'0944

ISBN-13: 978-1-911667-82-7

Typeset by Palindrome
Cover design by Myriam Bell Design, UK
Printed and bound by Finidr, Czech Republic

Contents

Contents

Plates

Pages 97–112

Plates

About the Author

Manfred Ziegler was born 7 June 1908. He had a lifetime fascination with flight. At the age of eight, he wrote to Manfred Freiherr von Richthofen, the famous 'Red Baron', asking to be allowed to fly with him. Richthofen even replied, saying, 'Yes, we'll fly together!'

At 21, he took up glider flying and he also pursued his diving, becoming a core member of Germany's Olympic high-diving team. In 1932 and 1934 he was the student world high-diving champion at the world championships in Darmstadt and Turin.

When war broke out in 1939 he became a pilot in the Luftwaffe, and from 1943 until the war's end he was a flying instructor and flew the Me 163 with Erprobungskommando 16 (Operational Test Unit 16) and Jagdgeschwader 400 (Fighter Group 400).

Many of his experiences are related in his popular account published in Germany under the title *Raketenjäger Me 163*. Following early release from Soviet captivity after the war he re-established contact immediately with many former Me 262 pilots and his notes of these conversations made when memories were still fresh are the basis for the current volume.

Having returned to Berlin he continued to fly and write newspaper articles. In Berlin he guested as a high-wire walker with the Camilla Mayer circus troupe, walking the 24-metre high wire – without any prior training – for a newspaper article. He eventually became editor-in-chief of the *Flug-Revue* aviation monthly in Stuttgart and, as such, made his first supersonic flight in an English fighter aircraft in the spring of 1960.

Author's Foreword

Dear Friends and Comrades!

This foreword is for all of you who flew the Me 262, whether as fighter pilot or bomber crew. I have been motivated to write this book for three reasons:

1 At present, the Me 262 and its history have received only a fragmented treatment in the literature of military aviation.
2 All previous narratives either gloss over the development stage of the Me 262, which was an ongoing event from the initial drawing board sketch to the last dogfight, or present an incomplete history within a biography of the aircraft.
3 The younger generation – my primary concern – has at best a very superficial understanding of the great drama surrounding the world's first operational jet fighter, which also served as the first bomber of its kind in aviation history.

Many young people have the idea that German fighter pilots – 'the collar-and-tie brigade' – were more given to boasting of their early victories instead of getting into the air to shoot down the Allied bomber formations. This is a misconception which needs to be corrected. Accordingly I have depicted what it was like to be on fighter operations, and for the benefit of the younger generation have thought it worthwhile to describe the experience of fighter action, something beyond their imagining.

During the lifetime of the frontline Me 262 I was an Me 163 test pilot and instructor, and so do not write as a jet-fighter pilot from my own immediate experience. The foundation for this book has therefore been a thorough research of the existing literature. To my comrades-in-arms of that epoch who placed themselves at my disposal for hours, and all night if need be, I offer my heartfelt thanks. I record their names in the Acknowledgements. No less are thanks due to the named firms of the German aviation industry.

In this volume I have paid no heed to rank or position and have tried to set aside old unresolved grudges, although here and there some subjectivity is bound to have crept in. Unavoidable too are the many gaps in the story which still remain. Therefore I shall be grateful to every comrade-in-arms – and every historian – who puts me right.

None of the praiseworthy efforts to compile the Me 262 story in the immediate postwar period succeeded. Despite there being many more relevant documents extant in the UK and US national archives than in the German Federal Republic, English language works are not free of error. American military aviation historians – and their British counterparts – have the advantage of easier access to sources for research. Seized by the victors were plans, drawings, reports, photographs, films, memoranda, diaries and they have much other additional useful material including PoW interrogation statements. These huge files have probably still not been fully evaluated to the present day. Much of the material has been returned to the German Federal Republic by the United States, to a much lesser extent by the British authorities. Precisely why the British want to keep secret what they have – not even allowing it to be worked from under supervision – is not known. All the documentation respecting the highly interesting organisation of the German night-fighter network under Generalleutnant Kammhuber remains in British hands. All attempts to date to obtain at least copies for the German military archives have been unsuccessful. It is all the more incomprehensible because the return of the material would not be against the interests of any nation but rather of inestimable value for historical research.

It will be a great success of this book if it inspires the Old Guard to criticise and correct me, or supply some missing pieces. I encourage it with a hearty 'Horrido!' – Into battle!

MANO ZIEGLER, GERMANY, 1978

Acknowledgements

The author is indebted to the following personalities for their assistance in compiling this book:

Horst Amberg
Hubert Bauer
Heinrich Beauvais
Hans-Ekkehard Bob
Dr Ludwig Bölkow
Wolfgang Degel
Hans J. Ebert
Georg Eder
Dr Anselm Franz
Karl Frydag
Adolf Galland
Gordon M. Gollob
Hajo Herrmann
Ludwig Hofmann
Erich Hohagen
Hans Hornung
Josef Kammhuber
Hans-Joachim Klein
Rakan Peter Kokothaki
Alfred Krüger
Willi Laughammer

Karl W. Lüttgau
Georg Madelung
Willy Messerschmitt
Friedrich Karl Müller
Edu Neumann
Ernst Obermaier
Dietrich Peltz
Edgar Petersen
Dr Viktor Emanuel Preusker
Jean Roeder
Karl Schnörrer
Rudolf Schoenert
Günter Sengfelder
Rudolf Sinner
Wolfgang Späte
Kurt Tank
Hannes Trautloft
Erich Warsitz
Günther Wegmann
Fritz Wendel
Heiner Wittmer

1

Fritz Wendel – A Test Pilot Possessed

T he parachute hanging loosely from his shoulders slapped the back of his knees and looked a couple of sizes too big for him. His ground technician suggested he ought to shorten the straps. Fritz Wendel waved him aside; it was too much bother. When he had dressed for the first flight before dawn that morning it had been bitterly cold, and he had worn his thick fur-lined combinations. The ridge of high pressure brought a cloudless April day. The sun had risen and beneath the azure sky it had grown pleasantly warm. Some cumulus began to form during the afternoon by when it was decidedly too hot for furry combinations and he had discarded them in favour of his lightweight flying overall. Hence the loose parachute. Four o'clock was late in the day for a test pilot who still had a couple more flights scheduled. So he had to get a move on.

The aircraft climbed. He had time to rehearse the drill mentally during the ascent to 18,000 feet. From there at full throttle he would put the fighter into a 'steep incline' as the manual called it. A works pilot ferrying in the first series of this particular machine had reported that at high speeds unpleasantly strong wing vibrations developed. The aircraft was a Bf 109T. The T stood for *Träger* (carrier), for this was one of the fighters designed to fly from the flight deck of Germany's aircraft carrier *Seydlitz*, an *Admiral Hipper*-class heavy cruiser hull being converted into a flat-top at a Baltic shipyard.

Compared with her sister aircraft, the Bf 109T had broader

wings and that was suspected to be somehow the cause of the unusual vibrations. Exactly how that caused the problem remained to be established. Possibly it would need no more than a couple of flights to identify the fault, as was often the case, or even only one. In five or six minutes he would know.

Yet it was with the new aircraft, the Me 262, that he had allowed himself to become preoccupied. The airplane which would become the world's first jet fighter once the turbines were delivered stood in the experimental hangar below, due to make her maiden flight in a few days – and he, Fritz Wendel, would be at the controls. She might have only a piston engine and spinner for the time being, but nothing would keep him away from her. In anticipation he savoured this step into a new epoch of aviation history.

At twenty-four years of age, Wendel was already the holder of the absolute world speed record, and had brought the propeller-driven aircraft as far as it could go. He didn't claim all the credit of course, naturally some rubbed off on Professor Willy Messerschmitt and his magnificent design and construction team. It was a joy to fly for an aircraft manufacturer who recognised no boundaries when a question of progress was involved.

At 18,000 feet Wendel levelled out and looked below. He could see the extensive Messerschmitt works, nearby the angular mosaic of Augsburg with the narrow alleys of the Fuggerei inside the town. Beyond all the houses and factories lay fields, woodland and mountains – the broad hump of the Zugspitze and the bizarre rocky mass of its neighbours.

Instruments OK? Everything ready! Throttle forward, nose down and he went into the dive at full revs. As the bird hurtled earthwards he heard the roaring engine, the howl of the slipstream and watched the speedometer needle rise – 600–650–700 kph. Through the cumulus. Now the needle indicated 750. Almost his own world record! He detected nothing out of the ordinary, a few vibrations certainly but harmless, caused by disturbed air below the cumulus. That was normal.

At 3,000 feet he pulled out and climbed to 22,500 feet for a second dive. He had to be certain that the works pilot had merely encountered turbulence below cloud and misinterpreted the effect.

Fritz Wendel – A Test Pilot Possessed

On the second dive the machine had just passed the 750 kph mark at 9,000 feet when the left wing, contorting, began to vibrate violently. The frequency of the vibration was so powerful that the whole aircraft shook. The contours of the wing blurred and only the rapid wave-like motion of the wing-tip could be distinguished. Nothing more could be done. He pulled back the throttle, unbuckled his seat straps and in the same split second it happened. The wing bent, its metal skin peeled off, ribbons of debris whipped away followed by the wing itself, snapped off at the joint with the fuselage. Scarcely a second had elapsed.

The remains of the Bf 109 fighter began to spin wildly as it careered groundwards. Somewhere there was another crack. Not that they were any use now, but he noticed how the controls were slack. As if in a centrifuge he was forced back into the leather seat, imprisoned by the irresistible G-force. His nerve held and his mind was clear. He had gone through the same thing a year before. A good 6,000 feet still separated him from the ground. He tried to prise himself up against the cabin sides. It cracked again somewhere. His hand could not reach the lever to throw off the plexiglass hood. The right wing broke off, the aircraft nose jerked down, he levered the cabin hood open and the force catapulted him out, spinning his body through the air like rag doll, sucking out his breath. He saw the ground swirling below him. It was nothing new, he belonged up here.

Wendel spread his arms and legs to brake the speed of his fall. The tremendous velocity began to ebb away as air resistance took effect. Seconds later quiet fell, and he experienced a sense of weightlessness in the vertical descent. Twenty-one feet per second, 1,250 feet per minute. And a minute is a long time between life and death. But now he would survive, would carry on living to fly again.

His hand felt for the rip cord to open the parachute. It was supposed to be on the left side between hip and shoulder, but his fingers located neither the steel ring nor the strap to which it was attached. His fingers began to feel, to search, more hastily. They found only the smooth fabric of his overall.

He took fright. Suddenly he remembered the loose straps which he had not bothered to adjust before taking off. He felt for the parachute pack, found it together with the dangling webbing which had slipped from his shoulder and now hung below his left hip. He replaced it correctly, looked down, gauging that he still had sufficient altitude, waited two or three seconds and then pulled the D-ring. The wire cable jerked free a steel pin from its retaining bracket and so released the silk. It was as easy as that to stay alive.

The canopy came free with a rustle, flapped, deployed normally, tipped him upwards and swung him. And then he saw coming directly towards him – twisting and turning like the wings of a lime-tree seed – the starboard wing of his broken Bf 109, which had separated in one piece from the fuselage. If this piece of spinning junk hit him or tangled into the parachute shroud lines it would not be the first time that a pilot had lost his life to such a freak occurrence just when all seemed safe. There was nothing he could do now but wait… The wing hissed by a few yards below his feet. He landed in a ploughed field and when checking himself over noticed the blood for the first time. He had lacerations to his face and a foot. Not bad, but a nuisance.

At the hospital the foot injury had to be stitched. The ankle needed to be immobilised: bedrest was prescribed. The doctor spoke of two to three weeks: the piston-engined Me 262 maiden flight was listed for three days hence. If he wasn't available it would be given to somebody else. There he lay, Fritz Wendel, undisputed holder of the world speed record, brimming with health and confined to bed.

In his hospital cot there was plenty of time for reflection. His mind wandered to the year 1938 when he first heard of the new machine which eventually would fly without a propeller and faster than his record-breaking machine, the Me 209 V1. For three years he had waited and watched almost paternally over the development of the new warbird, had pored over the blueprints, chatted with the engineers and later had often spent hours in the experimental hangar noticing how this piece or that was fitted to her. And now, from his hospital bed, he would be forced to put a brave face on it and listen to a colleague's joyous account of what it had been like to fly his personal baby…

He spoke to the medic, who shrugged his shoulders. When the

superintendent of the experimental hangar visited his bedside, Wendel begged him to delay the flight. The superintendent promised to do what he could. Privately he thought the man must be crazy, wanting to hobble from his hospital bed to fly a jet fighter airframe fitted with a piston engine and propeller. Wendel settled back, hands behind his head on the pillow. His mind was restless, but his thoughts always came back to when it began…

2

Messerschmitt AG Developments
1926–41

After joining the Bayerische Flugzeugwerke as a young management assistant in 1926, Rakan Peter Kokothaki worked his way up through the organisation to become eventually the Member for Finance and Marketing on the Messerschmitt AG board. In 1928 Willy Messerschmitt had moved his small aircraft building business from Bamberg to Augsburg, integrating it into the Bayerische Flugzeugwerke but retaining for his design offices a measure of autonomy from the larger firm. Kokothaki thus became an interested observer at first hand of Messerschmitt's relentless lust for aircraft designing from 1928 onwards.

A year before the move, Messerschmitt had developed the M 20, a ten-seater commercial aircraft. Deutsche Lufthansa, controlled at the time by Erhard Milch, later to become Goering's Luftwaffe Secretary of State, ordered ten of the machines. Appointed as test pilot for the maiden flight at Augsburg on 26 February 1928 was Hans Hackmack, Erhard Milch's personal friend and pilot. The flight took a most tragic course. Hubert Bauer, then an assistant at the works, later a Messerschmitt AG board member of long standing, was a witness to the accident and described it thus:

> The aircraft flew for a considerable time over the aerodrome and surrounding district without any problems. After about twenty minutes it came back over the airfield and through binoculars one could see something bright flapping at the

trailing edge of a wing. Shortly we saw the pilot emerge from the door at the rear of the fuselage and jump. His parachute canopy began to deploy immediately and tangled into the aircraft so that Hackmack was left dangling by the parachute straps. While he struggled desperately to unsnag it by tugging on the shrouds and kicking out, the aircraft continued serenely in level flight for quite some time before eventually the nose dipped and dived into the ground. Hackmack was killed instantaneously.

The investigation reported that some fabric had come loose at the trailing edge and this was the flapping seen by witnesses. It was assumed that the pilot had mistaken it for a fire or believed that the wing had fractured. Nobody was directly responsible for the accident. Hans Hackmack had probably lost his nerve, perhaps mindful of a test flight a few weeks previously in which he had narrowly escaped death. According to the report there should have been no problem landing the M20 safely.

That Milch was deeply affected by the death of his friend was obvious. He blamed nobody but reacted very emotionally at Messerschmitt's disinterest in his personal loss. Messerschmitt did not even deign to attend the crash site. This coldness in Messerschmitt's personality was one of the causes for the split in the relationship between them.

Nevertheless Milch ordered two modified M20a aircraft after they had been test-flown and pronounced problem-free. They proved successful on operations and when an M20b version became available Lufthansa also ordered two of these. Both crashed, one with only the pilot aboard, but the other involved passenger deaths. Initially, Messerschmitt was accused of having built M20b in breach of safety regulations but after examining both wrecks, the German Test Institute for Aviation (*Deutsche Versuchsanstalt für Luftfahrt*) rejected the accusations. The actual cause was put down to sudden turbulence. Little was known of this at the time although aeronautical scientists in Germany were studying the phenomenon.

Willy Messerschmitt – today an acknowledged pioneer of lightweight construction – spared weight wherever possible provided it did not contravene aircraft construction regulations. If the regulations themselves were inadequate, that was not his fault. The two M 20b accidents were thereafter always known as the 'Turbulence Cases'. How widely known Messerschmitt had become for his successful lightweight airframes is exemplified by the following anecdote: The Academic Pilot Group (*Akademische Flieger- gruppe*) Berlin had ordered from Augsburg the sporty M 23. The Group's leader, a Dr Leander, arrived at Augsburg to fly the aircraft to Berlin. Messerschmitt took this important client for a guided tour of the works and rounded off by asking if the customer had any request. 'Yes,' Leander said, 'Show me how you scrape the wood off from beneath the varnish.'

The consequence of the three M 20 crashes was the cancellation of the Deutsche Lufthansa order. This meant administration for the Bayerische Flugzeugwerke. The negotiations were handled between Augsburg banker Friedrich Seider, an experienced liquidations administrator, and the BfW financial wizard Kokothaki, and lasted from 1931 until the Hitler government saved the firm with the first armaments contracts in 1933. Kokothaki despaired at the construction costs incurred from early on by Messerschmitt. Although the aircraft were outstanding, demand was slack. But Messerschmitt was not the only aircraft builder who paid scant heed to costs so long as others were going to be paying them.

During the Spanish Civil War another Messerschmitt design, the Bf 109 fighter, confirmed a superiority which had been self-evident for some time and in the summer of 1937 the Bf 109 left the aviation world in shocked silence. Dübendorf aerodrome near Zürich was the venue for an international flying tournament attended by entrants from France, Italy, Germany, Britain, Czechoslovakia and elsewhere. There were five competitions and the Bf 109 won all five. The machine flew and climbed faster than all its rivals. As a fighter it won the individual and team races. Never before had German aircraft even participated in an international competition. A few in the know might have been confident enough to place a bet on one or two victories. Europe was already bracing itself for war. To win all five races outright was almost a provocation. The Bf 108 *Taifun* four-seater pleasure aircraft, and

the Bf 109 fighter, his two excellent designs, elevated Willy
Messerschmitt and his engineers, who numbered among the best in
Germany, into the front rank of the world's aircraft builders.

In the spring of 1938, they now faced a daunting task. Men who
would later become household names in Germany – Lusser, Voigt,
Degel, Hornung, Kaiser, Wackerle and Ludwig Bölkow, a young
graduate engineer fresh from University who knew his subject, had
talent and a store of ideas – wrestled at desk and drawing board
with the mathematics and technical design of an aircraft which was
certain to lead them into virgin territory. The problem confronting
the team was to come up with something special in aircraft design.
A machine to succeed the Bf 109 no less, and that was by no means
going to be easy. Within a few months they had conceived project
P 1065 for a twin-engined jet fighter. The files entitled 'Me 262 –
Pursuit Fighter' were presented to the Reich Air Ministry on 7 June
1938. Six months afterwards, in December 1938, engineers and
officials from the Ministry made their first inspection of the full-
size mock-up. The contract for the construction of three
experimental aircraft followed a little later.

Elsewhere a series of world records was now set and broken. On
11 November 1937 – shortly after Dübendorf – Dr Hermann
Wurster, chief test pilot of the Bayerische Flugzeugwerke, the trade
name of the Messerschmitt organisation, hence 'Bf', reached
611.004 kph in a souped-up Me 109E. The flight set a world record
for land aircraft. On Whit Sunday 1938 the World War I fighter ace
Ernst Udet flew at 634.73 kph over 100 kilometres at the controls
of a Heinkel He 100, easily destroying the existing record of 554
kph held by the Italian Francesco Agello. On 30 March 1939 Hans
Dieterle flying the Heinkel He 100 V8 set an absolute world speed
record with 746.606 kph which Messerschmitt test pilot Fritz
Wendel broke in turn on 26 April 1939 with 755.138 kph.

Wendel's machine was not a souped-up Bf 109, from which it
differed outwardly, but an aircraft designed specifically to set the
world record, the Me 209 V1. It was shorter, had finer wings; the
Bf 109 water-cooling system with its high frontal resistance had
been replaced by a surface-mounted radiator and an evaporation
device; the oil cooler was a circular intake set in the airstream

behind the propeller. Seven litres of cooling water were consumed per minute. Propulsion was supplied by an 1,800 hp DB601 V10 12-cylinder liquid-cooled piston engine specially engineered by Daimler–Benz for record attempts and could manage 2,770 hp in a five-minute burst. The record was claimed at the Fédération Aéronautique Internationale (FAI) for an aircraft designated Me 109R to give the impression for propaganda purposes that a modified Me 109 had taken the world record. No effort was spared to protect the machine from the camera to maintain the deception.

The expression 'the Me 109' sounds more formidable and slips off the tongue more smoothly than 'Bf 109' and the Propaganda Ministry was quick to seize upon it. The deception was never corrected with the FAI and Fritz Wendel's world record stood for thirty years. Even then only a few surpassed it. In 1939 Germany had four pilots who each held a world aviation speed record, and that in itself was a world record.

These achievements brought the piston engine to the zenith of its development. The four-stroke machine invented by Nikolaus August Otto could advance no further. And aircraft speeds could neither be increased by higher revs or a different design of spinner. To fly faster would only be possible powered by rockets or jet propulsion. In the endurance field, hardly 500 kph had been attained: even the Me 109 could not manage 400 kph in winning the competition over the set course at Dübendorf. The fastest propeller-driven aircraft of World War II were the twin-engined RAF Mosquito, and the German Dornier 335 '*Pfeil*' with a propeller front and rear. These were capable of approaching 750 kph in December 1944 and became the world's fastest series-produced aircraft. But that was the dead end.

The first manufacturer to fly a jet aircraft successfully was Ernst Heinkel AG of Warnemünde, whose experimental rocket-propelled He 176 and jet-propelled He 178 made their maiden flights piloted by Erich Warsitz in the summer of 1939. Interested onlookers on the ground were Hitler, Goering and Ernst Udet, Minister for Aircraft Production and Supply, but with the impending invasion of Poland only weeks away decisions had to be postponed until such time as Warsaw had requested an armistice. The German High

Command was sure that Britain and France would look the other way once more. Later in the war both aircraft went on show in the Berlin Aviation Museum and were eventually destroyed there in an air raid.

The successor to the He 178 was the twin-engined He 280 with He S 8A turbines each developing 700 kg thrust. First tested in 1942, Udet recognised the possibilities of the machine at once but his pleas for its adoption by the Luftwaffe fell on deaf ears. Seven months later he was dead and Milch, who took over his office, lacked his predecessor's vision and felt that the development of the turbojet 'with which the He 280 was first powered had enough bugs in it that the original flights of the jet fighter were made with the engines uncowled' and was thus not sufficiently advanced for him to advocate it. In the event, although work was continued on the prototype, the aircraft fell prey to the 1940 edict that any development which would not be usable within six months was to be abandoned. This might not have stopped Professor Messerschmitt but it was certainly the end of the He 280, the aircraft for which the time was ripe.

Shortly before the outbreak of war, aeronautical engineers in Britain, France, Italy and the United States were considering jet-engine designs, but in development already they lagged far behind Germany. The Kiel-based firm of Hellmuth Walter supplied the 600 kg-thrust rocket motor for the Heinkel He 176 and was developing a liquid fuel for the Alexander Lippisch-designed Me 163 rocket fighter. The jet engine for the He 178 had been built by engineer Dr Hans Pabst von Ohain while early work on jet turbines had been in hand since 1935 at BMW and the Junkers Motorenwerke (Jumo). Information regarding progress being made on building the new turbines came from BMW and Jumo in a steady flow and Messerschmitt was confident that his Me 262 prototypes would be ready for testing as soon as the turbines arrived and were fitted.

Since BMW led Junkers in the development race, Messerschmitt consulted chiefly with the Bavarian firm and calculated from the available data that the fighter could top 800 kph in level flight. This speed was hitherto only dreamed of but still sufficiently short of the sound barrier that the expected problems at Mach 1 need not be addressed.

There was an initial difference of opinion about where the two engines should be sited. For aerodynamic reasons, Messerschmitt himself wanted the two cigar-shaped turbines built into the wings. After his engineers explained the difficulties this would cause, such as poor accessibility for maintenance and repair, the large personnel requirement for engine changes and finally a much greater risk of the whole aircraft exploding if hit by enemy fire, Messerschmitt was persuaded to sling a turbine below each wing. This would allow a conventional piston engine to be fitted in the nose of the experimental prototype as a stand-by in the event of turbine failure. The wisdom of this precaution was to prove itself, although not quite in the way that had been anticipated.

By the outbreak of war in September 1939, German military aviation had been developed only to the stage where the Luftwaffe could control the airspace over the Reich and the territories adjacent to it. Until then, it had seemed improbable that Germany would be faced by a dangerous enemy or superior combined enemy forces in the air. Hitler had concluded a non-aggression pact with the Soviet Union, the French air force was obsolete, the Polish air arm was small, obsolete and not independent of the Polish army, while Germany with 4,500 aircraft, some of them of the most modern design, led the field in Europe. The RAF at the time had a thousand fewer aircraft than the Luftwaffe.

The lightning victories over Poland and then France played their part in strengthening German confidence in the invincibility of the Wehrmacht and there were relatively few people, even among those in the know about certain adverse trends in Luftwaffe develop-ment, who took a less sanguine view. But even having disposed of the French, the German Luftwaffe was simply not strong enough for an air-war across the western European continent, particularly if pitted against the consequential and technically well-armed opponent which Great Britain was becoming. After an initial superiority the balance shifted to a parity between the fighter pilots of both sides during the Battle of Britain, but Germany lacked a modern heavy bomber able to penetrate far enough inland with a worthwhile payload even from airfields in northern France. And had such a bomber been available, no fighter existed with the range to provide aerial protection to, say, Liverpool or the Tyne and back. Early on, all hopes resided in the He 177 bomber. This machine was to prove itself a problem child of the first order. The trio of twin-engined bombers which formed the backbone of the German offensive against southern England were short-ranged and either troublesome mechanically, such as the Ju 88, or obsolete, as were the He 111 and Do 17: the Bf 110 'destroyer' was too slow and had little value as a bomber. The mediocrity of the Bf 110 had been recognised by the Reich Air Ministry in 1939. Udet himself had asked Messerschmitt if he would be able to supply the Luftwaffe with 2,000 improved Bf 110s by October 1942. Messerschmitt said yes and got the contract. This meant that he was now turning out Germany's principal fighter, and soon would be responsible for producing Germany's principal light bomber, and after that the world's first jet fighter.

By the beginning of 1941 – still without the jet turbines – the airframes of Me 262 prototypes V1, V2 and V3 were reported to the Ministry as ready for aerial testing. Since the manufacturers could not confirm a delivery date for the new turbines, Messerschmitt decided to fit a 750 hp Jumo 210G piston engine in the fuselage nose for the first test flights. Being portly, it was certainly a departure from the aerodynamic elegance of the shark-like hull, but it would serve its purpose and save time.

On the evening of 18 April 1941, Fritz Wendel, who had discharged himself from hospital against medical advice, climbed into the cockpit of Me 262 V1 and took off at 19:35 hrs. With its relatively weak engine, it was a close call to get the 2,660 kilos of machine into the air before arriving at the end of the 1,000-yard runway. In its first ascent and at altitude the new aircraft showed good flying qualities although the maximum 420 kph in level flight was only half its designed top speed. To see how the hull behaved at higher speeds, the aircraft had to be dived at a steep incline at full throttle repeatedly over the series of trials. On the first test, wing vibrations were observed at 540 kph. Twice previously flying other aircraft types Wendel had had to evacuate by parachute perilously close to the ground, but that was the risk a test pilot ran in the endeavour to find a new aircraft's defects if it was to be recommended for series production. As the angle of dive became ever steeper, the starting altitude became progressively higher to allow the pilot more time to bale out in case of disaster. Wendel established that the dangerous vibrations fell away at higher speeds. This brought him a certain relief, but he was sure that later when the jet powerplants were fitted and provided much higher speeds, more unpleasant surprises would be bound to lie in wait. The flight characteristics of the new hull were not merely good, however; stability, the effectiveness of flaps, ailerons and rudder and performance at slow speed in particular were outstanding. Test flying the Me 262 airframe lasted the remainder of 1941.

3

Shortages, Technical Difficulties and the First Me 262 Crash

The chronic shortage of aviation spirit and materials for aircraft construction forced stringent economies including the halting of new developments considered speculative or whose completion was too far off. The Luftwaffe had been led to expect that it had until 1942 to equip for a major confrontation but in the event Germany had the dreaded scenario of war on two fronts once the Wehrmacht made its incursion into Soviet Russia on 21 June 1941. The day before, Hitler had ordered a reduction in the army and naval budget in favour of Luftwaffe armaments. Immediately following the announcement Goering demanded that the strength of the Luftwaffe be quadrupled and empowered his Secretary of State, Generalinspekteur Erhard Milch, to carry out the special task of establishing the capacity of the German aviation industry.

Milch requested from Goering a written appointment as pleni-potentiary and received by return a document endowing him with unique scope. There was practically nothing which lay outside his jurisdiction from the closing down of factories to the building of new ones.

At that time aviation production was in a poor state and output was insufficient to cover combat losses. Factory managers blamed two factors: shortages of labour and aluminium. Milch had this allegation investigated and discovered scarce aluminium and aeronautical-quality sheet-plate was being diverted to non-aircraft processes. He also found that Udet had made a significant reduction in engine production and the output of bombers, particularly the He 111 and Ju 88, but that no new bomber type was scheduled for series production. Even the Me 210, an improved version of the Bf 110, would not be operational before October 1942.

German intelligence was supplying horrendous reports regarding the rapidly growing production of aircraft in the still neutral United States and even Britain, where the factories were not disturbed by nightly enemy bombardment and could thus work at full output. Finally Milch learned that the new diveable bomber types would not be ready for operations before 1944.

By now very perturbed, Milch took Udet with him to visit Messerschmitt at Augsburg for the purpose of investigating the situation respecting the Me 109F fighter. Director Rakan Kokothaki had sources in Berlin close to Udet and Milch and knew that both were highly displeased that so few fighters were rolling off the production line. They were most anxious for the new Me 109F with its Daimler–Benz 605 engine, which was still causing serious problems. Furthermore Kokothaki knew of Milch's exasperation at the succession of new aircraft types at Augsburg at such a critical time, of which as Milch understood it there were at the time no fewer than twelve being worked upon by designers and engineers. Upon notification of the forthcoming visit, Kokothaki recalled advising his chief: 'For God's sake, under no circumstances mention any project other than the Me 109F, and particularly not the Me 262.'

Milch and Udet arrived at the works on 7 August 1941. When awkward questions were posed at the very beginning of the tour of inspection about the series production of the Me 109F, Messerschmitt led his guests into another hall where he showed them Me 262 V1. He was convinced that at the first sight of the wonder aircraft they would forget the Me 109F. Milch went red in the face. His small mouth with its narrow lips pursed for a moment into an almost invisible line. Then he demanded, 'What is the meaning of this, gentlemen? I have not come here to listen to music of the future but to find out how long you are going to keep us waiting to get the Me 109F operational. You are to concern yourselves exclusively with aircraft which we need right now and not with prototypes whose engines are not yet properly in order!' (In August 1941, the 004A had just managed a thrust of 600 kilos with new turbine wheels on the Junkers test rig.) In connection with this directive, he ordered the head of his Ministry's aircraft construction monitoring office to ensure that work on the Me 262 was halted at once and all energies focused on a production line for the Me 109F.

Udet stood aside during this scene, lurking in the background in a silent rage. Not until the leave-taking in the administration building did he make his bitter reproaches to Kokothaki regarding the desolate condition of the works. Everything was in pieces and the whole thing was a shambles, he said. Then he rejoined Milch's entourage for the return flight to Berlin. There is evidence that in the long period preceding the Augsburg visit Milch and Messerschmitt had actively sought a reunion. It was at Milch's suggestion that Messerschmitt was nominated a Professor. The negative result of the inspection was the final straw for Milch in the relationship with Messerschmitt, and the same was true for Kokothaki. But far, far worse was to follow.

It will be recalled that in 1939, Udet had awarded Messerschmitt a contract to provide, by October 1942, 2,000 light bombers of the designation Me 210, an improved version of the Bf 110. This situation now led directly to the most incomprehensible error of judgement in the history of world aircraft production. Perhaps overconfident because of his great personal ability and the Messerschmitt company's track record, but also on account of the very short delivery date, Messerschmitt set up the jigs for series production and made a start turning out the airframes before the Me 210 maiden test flight. The latter was by all accounts the most hair-raising twenty minutes in the career of chief test pilot Hermann Wurster, who returned from it alive thanks only to his outstanding ability as a flier. 'The aircraft is so unstable that it cannot be mass-produced in its present configuration. You couldn't trust any pilot's life to it. Apart from other modifications, the fuselage needs to be a metre longer,' he reported. Faced with this damning opinion from his chief test pilot, Messerschmitt had to decide between losing many millions of Reichmarks or closing his eyes to the major problem and making do with the minor changes. He settled for the latter. After five Me 210 test pilots from the Luftwaffe's experimental base at Rechlin had been given a decent burial, it was accepted that Dr Wurster was correct. Series production of the Me 210 was halted by the Reich Air Ministry on 13 March 1942 by which time 483 operationally useless machines had been completed.

The major change to the airframe was now no longer possible on the grounds of time alone. The financial loss to Messerschmitt AG was estimated at around RM 40 million (a labourer's annual wage at the time was about RM 1,500). Enormous sums had to be paid to the suppliers of materials, fitments, equipment and instruments. Scarce raw materials from partially completed aircraft were piled into great mountains of scrap in large warehouses. The loss in aircraft production and valued members of the workforce completed the blow for the Augsburg works, which in peacetime would have been bankrupted. Messerschmitt was relieved of his position as company head and retained only as a technical director.

Naturally, no effort was spared to convert and modify the design into a safer, better aircraft. The result was the Me 410 'fast bomber' with a top speed of 590 kph which could carry a one-tonne pay-load and was gunned-up as a destroyer aircraft. There was a corresponding reconnaisance version. It was a decent aeroplane certainly, but not one which lived up to the high expectations one had of a Messerschmitt.

Udet committed suicide four months after the Augsburg visit. The grandiose fighter ace of the Great War, the unsurpassable pilot and daredevil aerobatic flier, the man who loved life, it was never within his capabilities to adjust to the hard realities of a high office of state. To blame Udet alone for all the inadequacies, errors of judgement and neglect is unjust. In the Luftwaffe pecking order Udet was below Goering and Milch, and he was the only one who really cared nothing for career and power. He had lived his life as an aviator. The future held only humiliation for him and the loss of his freedom. Therefore he chose to go.

Willy Messerschmitt had no intention of abandoning work on the Me 262 in the wake of Milch's visit. A few days afterwards he had discussed his situation with Senior Engineer Meyer, head of the monitoring office, and found him sympathetic. All held the view that nothing useful would be served by bringing work on the aircraft to an abrupt halt, for it was making no demands on production capacity nor consuming large quantities of materials. Therefore Meyer agreed to turn a blind eye to no more than two dozen engineers continuing to work on the project.

It was the winter of 1941 before a pair of 003-TL turbines arrived from BMW Berlin-Schönefeld. Once fitted, the ground rolling trials lasted into March 1942. Fritz Wendel familiarised himself with the construction, operation and maintenance of the new engines both during these running trials and also with Junkers at Dessau and BMW. To safeguard the test pilot against all eventualities in the air the central piston engine with spinner would be retained. This motor required its own fuel tank and the back-up system made the aircraft very heavy but it was decided not to take the chance that the new jet engines would provide a trouble-free performance first time out.

In high spirits on 25 March 1942 Wendel carefully pushed the two throttle levers to full power, released the brakes and let the Me 262 roll forward. During the first minute all went well. It was immediately obvious that the aircraft needed more than a 1,000-yard runway but just short of the airfield fence the machine rose quickly to 150 feet. As Wendel was retracting the undercarriage the left jet stopped, quickly followed by the other. A jet aircraft configuration cannot glide and without the piston engine in the nose the aircraft would have fallen to the ground with little hope of survival for the pilot. As it was, Wendel was able to maintain his low height, make a careful circuit and land safely. An engine survey revealed that the compressor blades of both turbines had failed. They were fractured, torn, bent, wrenched from their sockets, had glowed with heat. It was a failure of materials. Materials which had been expected to be, but were not, adequate for the task they were called upon to do. This was not something merely irremediable overnight; there were no basics to go back to, for no prior flight data existed. The test rig in the BMW factory and running trials at Augsburg had proceeded satisfactorily and therefore the failure of both turbines simultaneously was apparently inexplicable. What was not understood at the time was the extent to which scientific research and practical experimentation into materials was necessary to make jet engines as safe as they are for modern commercial passenger-carrying aviation today.

BMW's engineers retired to Berlin-Schönefeld with their ruined turbines and it would be a long time until they were heard from again. Whether the project would have survived had not the Jumo 004A powerplant reached the completion stage at Junkers Motorenwerke is a moot point. As with BMW, Junkers had also received a contract from the Reich Air Ministry to develop a jet engine. Leading a team of specialist engineers, Dr Herbert Wagner, Head of Development at Junkers, had embarked on the task in 1935. Four years later work began building the 004A.

Von Ohain, with his jet engine for the He 178, and the British designer, Whittle, used radial compressors; Junkers and BMW preferred an axial construction with a smaller frontal surface more suitable for higher air speeds. Dr Anselm Franz, who was responsible for jet-engine development at Junkers at the time and after the war was appointed Vice-President of the Avro–Lycoming Division, Stratford (USA), wrote in 1967:

Taken as a whole, the 004 jet bears great similarity to the modern jet engine. It consisted of an eight-stage axial flow compressor, six single combustion chambers, a single-stage axial turbine which drove the compressor and a jet with an adjustable needle which was built from the beginning for the later addition of an after-burner. A special regulator had been developed which at higher revolutions kept the selected revolutions and the corresponding gas temperature constant automatically. This regulator was mounted together with other equipment on the upper side of the compressor housing. The starter motor was located in the compressor intake hub. The contract specified a thrust of 600 kg at full throttle, but a large reserve was expected. The design of the Jumo 004A was completed in the spring of 1940 and the engine first ran on the test-stand on 11 October 1940. Full revolutions were achieved in December that year and it was run at 430 kg thrust in January 1941. Cracks in the compressor blades caused by vibration then brought the test-stand development to a halt. The designed thrust of 600 kg was reached in August 1941 following modifications to turbine wheel construction. In December the same year the engine was run for ten hours, 1,000 kg thrust being obtained. Apart from the vibration problem mentioned earlier, few other basic flaws came to light in the development and testing of the 004A. After these extremely promising results the Reich Air Ministry contracted for eighty units of 004A for further development and operational testing.

Procuring the high-value and rare materials to progress the 004 development presented special difficulties. Tricks-of-the-trade and improvised solutions had to be employed in order to proceed at all. Dr Franz continues:

The 004A engine was an experimental rig. For that reason and because of the scarcity of certain valuable materials in Germany at the time – heat resistant materials such as nickel, molybdenum and cobalt were simply not available – it was unsuitable for mass production. To mass-produce the Jumo 004B required a far-reaching, radical reappraisal of the situation. As an example I would mention that sheet-plated areas such as the combustion chambers and thrust jet were adapted to take the normal steel plate flw 1010, the surfaces being protected against rust by a layer of aluminium. Special air-cooling measures were necessary to keep the temperature of the plating within acceptable limits. The production-line 004B had a thrust at take-off of 910 kg. On tests beginning in the summer of 1943, fractures were found in the turbine blades. This was due to a resonance between the vibration count of the blades and the vibrations occurring in the six combustion chambers at maximum revolutions. To save time we often resorted to unusual methods. In this particular case I recall well the professional musician with the perfect ear brought in expressly to determine the individual vibration count of each turbine wheel blade by use of a tuning fork. This method was successful. After a short, rather tense period, the difficulties were overcome substantially by a slight increase in the vibration count of the blades and a corresponding reduction of the maximum revolutions count from 9,000 to 8,700 revs per minute...

Dr Franz's report highlights the Achilles' heel of the jet engine in the development stages: the material of which the turbine wheel blades were manufactured. They were required to withstand a very high degree of heat and revolved at enormous velocity. It remained an awkward snag in jet engine development years after the war. One cannot praise highly enough the success of the Junkers Motorenwerke people in solving such problems under the adverse circumstances of the time. Although there were occasional breakdowns, they occurred relatively seldom in the operational career of the Me 262.

It is fair to assume that the problem defeated BMW's engineers. The failure of the two jet engines on the first test flight was in no way attributable to technical inadequacy on their part but rather to the absence of technical experience in a completely new field and the general shortage of materials in Hitler's Germany.

Four months had passed since the unsuccessful maiden flight of the V1 with a pair of inadequate BMW turbines. Meanwhile work had proceeded apace on prototypes V2 and V3 and these two aircraft had each received two Jumo 004A turbines. Despite the proven wisdom of the belt-and-braces approach, it had been decided to run the risk of pure jet flight. V1 had been relieved of its piston engine and none had ever been installed in the other two prototypes.

For security reasons but also because the runway was a hundred yards longer than at Augsburg, the V3 maiden flight took place at Leipheim. This was the aerodrome where the Messerschmitt *Giganten*, the Me 321 and 323, were flown and tested and security was very tight there.

Following the successful completion of the usual tests and rolling trials, 18 July 1942 was set for the first Me 262 jet flight.

Using results obtained from take-offs with the piston-engined V1, calculations had shown that with an all-up weight of five tonnes, V3 would leave the ground at a speed of 180 kph. It was known from runway trials using the jet powerplant that this speed was reached at a point about 800 yards from where the brakes were released. It left a reserve of only 300 yards from the end of the runway. This was not much, and – worse – on the rolling trials at between 170 and 180 kph, the V3 had so far shown no inclination to want to lift off!

All previous flights had been made with a propeller running. After hurtling down the runway on more occasions than he cared to count, Fritz Wendel had now determined the cause of the problem. Since there was no air stream from a spinner, the attitude of the upper wing was influenced by the strong slipstream behind it. This reduced the effectiveness of the flaps to the extent that when the aircraft was approaching its take-off speed, it had still not assumed the designed horizontal attitude. A nose wheel would solve the problem but it was out of the question to suspend the test programme while the two jet-engined prototypes were fitted with a retractable nose wheel, or a modified V4 built.

The reportedly unfavourable demeanour of the competent Reich Air Ministry officials towards what was beginning to look like a new type might perhaps have brought the whole project to an untimely conclusion. The rejection of the two perfectly viable Heinkel aircraft, including the He 178 jet, in August 1939 had not been forgotten and the scarcity of certain valuable materials was assuming worrying proportions. In short, there were plausible reasons for the gentlemen in Berlin to postpone the whole enterprise until after Final Victory had been achieved, an event of which all were still confident at the time. In the struggle between technology and politics lay the root of tragedy, as one would later discover.

Compared with great concerns of State in Berlin, the worries which preoccupied Leipheim were minor matters indeed, except to Wendel, who was now facing a challenge involving the question of his personal survival. During the deliberations as to how the Me 262 V3 tailplane could be elevated enough for take-off, the apparently absurd suggestion was put forward that at 180 kph and only 300 metres from the end of the runway, Wendel should step on the footbrake. If he got the pressure just right, it would get the tail up, at the same time raising the tail control surfaces out of the slipstream. The idea was logical and it would work, that was obvious. But it meant dicing with death.

If the pilot braked too hard at that speed, he risked somersaulting the aircraft. Even without full tanks his chances of survival would be slender. If on the other hand he applied the brakes too gently, the tailplane would not rise sufficiently and the ailerons would not escape the evil influence of the slipstream. Whatever he did next, he was bound to overshoot the runway end. Suddenly ploughing through a cornfield at 120 knots or so would require luck for survival. Those were the two alternatives which went alongside success; the odds were two-to-one on for disaster, and when the possibility of failure of one or both engines (as had happened previously) was thrown in for good measure, he reckoned his chances of survival as no better than 25 per cent. It was with this outcome in mind that at 08:40 hrs on 18 July 1942 he pushed the two throttle levers of V3 to maximum thrust.

300 yards from the runway end the pilot stabbed firmly but briefly at the footbrake. The nose of the jet dipped to the horizontal, the ailerons came into the airstream and the aircraft obeyed the stick. Just beyond the 900-yard mark the Me 262 rose into the air. The sharp whine of the Junkers jets remained constant and in his joy at the successful take-off, Wendel dismissed from his mind all the earlier difficulties. Instead of the robust, noisy piston engine squatting in the fuselage ahead of him to which he had become so accustomed, he heard only a soft rustling like a refreshing breeze. The control surfaces were slick to respond and the 5-tonne machine cruised like a bird carried on a thermal.

For a few seconds the pilot surrendered to this glorious sensation of carefree gliding. Remembering his duties, he noted that the instruments read normal, the aircraft felt comfortable and stable, sweet when trimmed. If he released his hold of the control stick the machine had a slight tendency to drift left, but that would be quickly ironed out once he landed. Seldom had Fritz Wendel been so satisfied, so lyrical, about a maiden flight. Yes, it was something to savour. In those days a maiden flight consisted of a single circuit around the town and every pilot was cock-a-hoop if everything went smoothly and no murderous dangers suddenly cropped up. After ten minutes in the air he was in the long drawn-out turn for a sedate approach to the airstrip. With jets throttled back, V3 sank slowly lower; the runway came ever nearer and without difficulty the wheels squelched. The flight had lasted twelve minutes in all. And then it was all jubilation: onlookers running from the airfield buildings, the groundstaff crowding round to offer their congratulations, an exultant Willy Messerschmitt.

An immediate conference involving Messerschmitt, his designers and the Junkers engineers followed the maiden flight. After an examination of the airframe and powerplant it was decided to adjust the control surfaces for trim and refuel the aircraft for a second flight. Wendel took off again just after midday and began a prescribed series of tests. On his return he reported that when banking steeply, the aircraft could not achieve a tight turn and the control stick felt heavy. The defect here seemed to lie in the wing design.

The Me 262 prototypes were built to an arrow-head plan in which the edges of the inner wing, i.e., from the wing root to the engine nacelle, were at a right angle to the fuselage. This part of the wing was exposed to high aerodynamic forces and the airflow spilled away too quickly. The swept-back configuration of the wings therefore only began at the outer engine casing.

The necessary modifications took about three weeks. The inner wing was broadened so that the whole wing was now swept back from the root. This gave the Me 262 its final form. The larger and more effective angle of attack provided the aircraft with a more acute turning radius and a slower landing speed, both crucial for fighter operations.

The Reich Air Ministry had been kept informed of progress, and at this point decided to appoint its own Luftwaffe test pilot. One of the most experienced was Heinrich Beauvais from the Rechlin Test Centre who telephoned Wendel and quickly agreed a date for the flight.

On the morning of 17 August 1942 Wendel escorted his guest

to the waiting V3 and spent a good half-hour providing his Rechlin colleague with a careful introduction to the cockpit. First he emphasised the absolute necessity to push the throttle levers forward slowly and cautiously and not with a jerk or brusque movement, because the turbines would stop at once and might catch fire. He demonstrated by moving the levers to show how he did it personally. He explained that after starting the engines, Beauvais should keep the brakes on, allowing the revs to mount slowly until they reached about 8,000 per minute. Then he should release the brakes, let the aircraft move forward and accelerate until the speedometer registered 180 kph. That would be at about the 800-yard mark. Wendel would position himself at the edge of the runway at that point so that Beauvais had a waymarker to know when he had to make the short stab at the brakes to get the tail up and so take off.

Beauvais got into the cockpit while Wendel drove to the 800-yard point. The tone of the V3's motors slowly swelled louder and he watched as the machine approached faster and faster towards him. The scene was now set for the accident which all had feared.

Wendel had the feeling as he watched the aircraft coming up that it was not moving fast enough. He dismissed the thought at once, for no irregularity was apparent from the howl of the jets nor could he estimate the actual speed of approach. It was 'just a funny feeling' but it made Wendel cry out 'Don't brake yet!' He watched in alarm as the Me 262 hurtled past, saw the tailplane rise and then sink back on the tail wheel almost immediately. The thunder of the jets deafening in his ears, Wendel stared horror-struck through the whirling dust as the rear of the aircraft rose up a second time and then subsided again about 150 yards further on.

The V3 was racing at full speed for the end of the runway. Wendel felt the urge to shut his eyes and so blot out the vision of the horrific disaster which now awaited Beauvais and could not be avoided. Spellbound he gazed after the speeding aircraft, had the impression that a last gallant effort was made to raise the tailplane before the Messerschmitt roared off the end of the runway into a cornfield where it was at once enveloped in an enormous cloud of dust.

Wendel heard a dull thump. He remained glued to the spot for a few seconds as he waited for the explosion, or for smoke to rise from the wreck. But below an expanding cloud of yellow-brown dust from the parched earth a deathly stillness reigned.

Wendel sprinted to his car and drove at full speed towards where Beauvais would be, still alive he hoped, perhaps seriously hurt, the best one could expect. He noticed on the other side of the airfield the fire appliances and ambulance also speeding to the accident site. It was mid-August, and a searing heat baked the plain at whose heart lay the Leipheim aerodrome, pasture and surrounding agricultural land. The ground was hard and dry and each of the vehicles trailed a yellowish plume of dust.

Wendel could not understand why the accident had occurred. Beauvais was a very good, reliable pilot, one of the best at the Luftwaffe Test Centre. He understood flight technology. He had tested many new aircraft and had trained himself to expect the unexpected. He was not the type of man who took off regardless, leaving it in the hands of Fate to deliver him and the aircraft back safely. He had flown many captured enemy aircraft transported to Rechlin for examination and had managed to survive without anybody giving him a thirty-minute briefing on the possible pitfalls.

At the controls of V3 he had not made an obvious error, and self-evidently he had applied the correct pressure to the brake at 800 yards since the tailplane had come up horizontally. 'Damn stupid braking,' Wendel thought and decided to do all he could to have all Me 262s fitted with a nose wheel. He could not leave operational pilots to guess their way through this accursed braking nonsense as he and Beauvais had done. The cornfield was bounded by a cart-track and halfway round he espied the accident site in an adjoining potato field. Beauvais was standing a few metres away from the ruined Me 262, which had come to a stop slewed broadside to the intended direction of flight. Both engines had been torn from their nacelles and lay aside from the main wreckage. Both wings were damaged, the right more than the left. The leg of the left wheel was bent, the right wheel had broken off. The aircraft was a mess but not irreparable.

As Wendel got out of his car, Beauvais could hardly suppress a grin at the expression on the Messerschmitt pilot's face. 'But

Beauvais, you're alive!,' Wendel cried, pumping his hand, slapping his back. 'You don't kill a weed so easily,' the Rechlin man responded, and stuck his left thumb into his mouth. 'You're injured, Beauvais?'

'I hurt my thumb on the throttle lever, but I don't need hospitalisation,' he explained, and returned the thumb to his mouth. 'So what went wrong then?,' Wendel demanded. Beauvais reflected for a few seconds. 'I've got no explanation other than this damned heat wave. As you saw, I got the wings up as I passed you. The aircraft was going slower than I expected but I thought the speed would build up OK by the time I got to you. I touched the brakes twice more afterwards as well.'

'And the revs were right?'

'Sure. When I released the brakes, both engines had 8,000, and the count didn't fall off during the run up. I think that the jets had too little thrust because of the outside air temperature – I can't think of another reason. When the aircraft didn't take off at the 800-yard mark, it seemed to me to be best to keep going in the hope that eventually she would rise… and the rest you know.'

'God only knows why you're here talking to me instead of the angels,' Wendel told him.

'After she roared off the airfield,' Beauvais continued, 'there was a sudden violent thump as if I had hit a ditch or something and that's what knocked the wheels off. After that she more or less finished the flight on her belly.'

'The ditch is actually a footpath across the cornfield, perhaps I should have warned you about it.'

Beauvais gave him a wry smile. 'I would still have hit it. After we slid to a stop I got out at once because one of the turbines was smouldering. With oil leaking out of the damaged fuel lines, I thought it best to observe from a respectful distance.' He thought for few moments and then concluded, 'If the first time I braked had been a bit later, say at 900 or 950 yards, when the speed was higher, probably I would have got up OK…'

As he finished speaking, one of the ambulance men arrived holding in his hand a very large potato, the V3 having ploughed up several furrows in her long slide across the dry land. 'Take good care of it,' he said to Beauvais, 'it's the first ever harvested by a jet aircraft.' Beauvais tossed the thick tuber into the air. 'Yes, I'm sure it is,' he replied, 'but what a damn stupid place the farmer chose to grow potatoes.'

4

A Fatal Crash and Hitler's Fatal Decision

After Beauvais' accident, it was 1 October 1942 before a V2, fitted with two Jumo 004 jets but still lacking a nose wheel, was ready to proceed with the programme of test flights. At 09:23 hours that day Fritz Wendel made a twenty-minute circuit over Augsburg, the first of numerous satisfactory flights with this particular aircraft which continued well into the spring of 1943. During this period there were no noteworthy occurrences.

Despite Milch's directive in August 1941 suspending all further work on the Me 262, it would appear that at some time in the succeeding year Reich Air Ministry contracts were placed with Messerschmitt AG for both the jet and the Me 163 rocket fighter. Milch himself remained sceptical and inflexible. After listening to Willy Messerschmitt deliver a report about progress on the Me 262 to a Development Conference at the Ministry of Aircraft Production on 13 November 1942, he refused to give the aircraft any financial support on the grounds that in view of the growing Allied air superiority over the Reich he wanted to concentrate on conventional fighter and bomber production.

The repaired V3 re-entered service for test flying in early April 1943 and Wendel as chief test pilot enlarged his flying team by the addition of a proven young colleague, Oberfeldwebel Wilhelm Ostertag. This was done with a view to shortening the period of Me 262 testing and have the machine in series production ahead of schedule.

After a few flights, Ostertag flew the V2 as well as Wendel. The problems with the powerplant appeared to be diminishing but had not yet been fully eradicated. Nevertheless, at Messerschmitt the time was considered ripe to discuss with the Ministry of Aircraft Production the question of an early start to series production, and the appropriate report was submitted to the Reich Air Ministry. The Berlin office despatched young Hauptmann Wolfgang Späte to Augsburg to fly the Me 262 and make his evaluation. He appeared a suitable man for the task, for he had been involved in the flight testing and preparation of the Me 163 for operations and had been selected to command the operational test unit Erprobungs-kommando 16. After his first Me 262 flight Späte wrote:

> What was immediately obvious was that this was a leap forward in aviation such that it was bound to bring us, as a nation at war, an unimaginable advantage, provided it was possible to produce the aircraft in time in sufficient numbers…

Continuing his test programme a few days later, he lost power in both engines at 9,000 feet. From an examination of the earlier flight data – principally in flying at slow speeds – it could be seen that he had throttled the engines back gradually to 2,000 revs. At the end of this experiment he attempted to regain thrust by pushing the throttle levers backwards and forward repeatedly, but neither engine responded, the rev counter remaining at 2,000. A brownish-black banner of smoke streamed astern from the jets.

The engines would not restart and after several more desperate attempts to regain control he had lost so much height that his only alternatives were abandoning the aircraft or crash-landing. Suddenly he recollected Wendel's instructions for such an eventuality. Wendel had once told him that in this predicament the thrust levers had to be restored to neutral and the engines restarted by the same procedure as if on the ground. At this juncture this advice was clearly not without its perils. If Wendel's advice was wrong, Späte would have lost so much altitude during the attempt that it would be too late to escape by parachute and he would be forced to crash-land. This might succeed but an explosion was a possibility.

43

Fortified by the philosophy 'Nothing is known for sure', Späte decided to stake all on Wendel.

Meanwhile the aircraft had sunk down to 4,500 feet and Späte had no more time to lose. Putting the thrust levers to neutral, he made an injection of fuel and pushed the left throttle very slowly forward. Suddenly there came the short explosive sound that was music to his ears, accompanied by an increase in speed which confirmed that the left turbine had ignited. The engine rev counter climbed to 4,500, a little later to full thrust.

The altimeter read only 1,350 feet, but already Späte no longer needed to concern himself with the question of baling out or crash-landing. On one engine he could maintain at least this height. The starboard engine responded similarly and he made a normal landing.

This extremely unsettling state of affairs for pilots was typical of what had to be endured when the powerplant of a new aircraft was not unconditionally reliable. Jet flight, particularly as regards the engines themselves, was still very much in its infancy. The works engineers had neither the necessary experience nor, as previously mentioned, access to the best materials. The investigation into Späte's almost disastrous flight came up with the explanation that if the Me 262 yawed when running at low revs, the strong lateral airflow could stop the compressor wheels and extinguish the ignition flame.

On 18 April 1943, the V2 was back in service. Späte drove with test-team leader Gerhard Caroli to the runway while the Me 262 was towed to the starting position by an aircraft-tug. This procedure was followed not only to save fuel but also to ensure that flying time was not reduced by wasting fuel taxiing to the runway.

At the starting position, Caroli offered Späte a cigarette. The two men conversed while smoking, eyeing the tug with the V2 in tow trundling slowly up the approach lane. When the aircraft arrived, Caroli signalled for his guest to get in, but Späte wanted to finish his cigarette (at the time cigarettes were rare in Germany). Just then a young test pilot, Wilhelm Ostertag, who was responsible for the maintenance of the V2, climbed into its cockpit and began to secure the straps of the aircraft's parachute pack over his shoulders.

When Späte made a questioning gesture to him from the ground, Ostertag pointed an index finger to his head as if to say 'I just want to check the machine over.'

Späte was annoyed but could hardly complain about the flight-sergeant's sense of duty and so he finished his cigarette while the V2 started up, took off and shortly disappeared below the horizon. Caroli, Späte, the ground technician and the tug driver waited patiently for Ostertag's return; it would not be more than twenty minutes before he reappeared. He had enough fuel for twenty-five minutes, but had to keep five minutes' worth in reserve in case the landing went awry and he had to go round again.

By the fifteen-minute mark they were watching the horizon with keen interest. After twenty minutes a certain disquiet had begun to creep in. After thirty-five minutes there could be no doubt but that Ostertag's flight had run up against some kind of snag. They revised the possibilities: emergency landing, baled out by parachute, landed at another airfield. Nobody wanted to suggest the fourth possibility.

Forty minutes had passed when the flight control vehicle came racing up the approach road to the starting point. A young man leapt out in haste. 'Are you missing a Ju 88?,' he shouted to Caroli. 'No, an Me 262,' Caroli answered, his face as white as chalk. 'You'd better follow me then!' The car sped back while Späte, Caroli and the technician bundled themselves aboard the slow aircraft-tug. Soon they knew the worst: young Ostertag had crashed. A vertical dive into the ground from 1,500 feet at full throttle.

The crash site was a deep crater with numerous scattered pieces of engine, ribbons of fuselage and bits of wing. The remains of Wilhelm Ostertag had already been collected by the ambulance people. Späte stood wordlessly before this picture of utter destruction. He had over one hundred kills to his credit as a fighter pilot and had seen dozens of such craters. He knew that any day it could be his turn. 'A few less puffs on a cigarette and they would have been picking bits of me out of there,' he muttered.

In May 1943 Späte and Willy Messerschmitt both contacted General der Jagdflieger Adolf Galland in Berlin, Späte to report his impressions of the new aircraft, Messerschmitt to invite Galland to fly the machine himself in the hope that it would inspire his advocacy in high places where it mattered and bring about the production of an Me 262 pre-series. He added that should the General obtain a positive feeling about the aircraft, perhaps he might then recommend to the Reich Air Ministry an order for one hundred. These could be delivered relatively quickly and would serve for conversion training and trials with operational units.

It was about this time that the idea became current – put forward in the main by Hitler himself – that the new jets should be used as bombers instead of as fighters. How this came about at a time when nothing was more urgent than an effective defence against enemy bombers will be explained in due course.

Galland accepted Messerschmitt's invitation and flew at once to Augsburg to try out the Me 262 for himself. In his book *Die Ersten und die Letzten* [The First and the Last] he described his first encounter with a jet aircraft:

> I will never forget the 22 May 1943 when I flew a jet aircraft for the first time in my life. Early that morning I met Messerschmitt at the Lechfeld experimental airfield near the Augsburg factory. Together with his aircraft designers, engineers and the Junkers engine specialists were the commander of the Rechlin Luftwaffe Test Station and the head of his fighter testing team, Behrens, killed shortly after the war in Argentina when he crashed a Pulqui II jet fighter. After introductory lectures by the expert engineers involved in the design, there was tense expectancy as we drove to the runway. There stood the two Me 262 jet fighters, the beginning and centrepoint of our future and at the same time our great hope. A strange sight, these aircraft without a propeller. Hidden in two streamlined cylinders below the airfoil were the jet turbines. None of the engineers could tell us exactly what horse-power they developed. In response to our questions they got busy with their slide rules and would only commit themselves to such-and-such hundred kilos of thrust at this and that airspeed at a given altitude which was equivalent at the corresponding flight weight to an expenditure of so much

horsepower airscrew propulsion. This made us piston-engine pilots very sceptical at first, for we were not yet tuned in to the peculiarities of this unknown thrust. But the engineers and their bizarre calculations were right. Essentially there really was no comparison with the power output for propellers. If the data they fed us, based on their calculations and to some extent already proven in flight, was even only more or less correct, then it opened up undreamed of possibilities. And everything depended on it!

The – at the time – fantastic speed of 850 kph in level flight meant a jump of at least 200 kph ahead of the fastest piston-engined fighter anywhere. Moreover, the aircraft could stay up from fifty to seventy minutes. For fuel it used a less costly diesel-type oil instead of the highly refined anti-knock kerosene which was becoming ever harder for us to obtain.

First the works chief test pilot demonstrated one of the two warbirds in flight. After it had been refuelled I climbed in. With numerous hand movements the mechanics started up the turbines. I followed the procedure with great interest. The first engine ran smoothly. The second caught fire. In a trice the turbine was in flames. Fortunately we fighter pilots are used to getting in and out of a cockpit rapidly. The fire was soon extinguished. The second Me 262 caused no problem. We set off down the 50-yard wide runway at ever increasing speed. I had no view ahead. These first jet aircraft were fitted with a conventional tail wheel in place of the nose-wheel gear which the type had in series production. Additionally one had to step on the brake suddenly. I thought, the runway is not going to be long enough! I was going at about 150 kph. The tailplane rose at last. Now I could see ahead, no more feeling that you are in the dark and running your head into a brick wall. With reduced air resistance the speed increased quickly. I was over 200 kph and some good way from the end of the runway when the machine took off benignly.

For the first time I was flying under jet power! No engine vibrations, no turning moment and no whipping noise from an airscrew. With a whistling sound my 'turbo' shot through the air. 'It's like having an angel push you,' I said later when asked what it was like. But war-conditioned, sober reality allowed me little time to savour the new experience of jet flight. Flight characteristics, turning ability, top speed, rate of climb – in just a few minutes I had to form an opinion of this new aircraft.

Just then the four-engined Messerschmitt [by this Galland must mean the prototype Me 264 transatlantic bomber then undergoing flight trials. *Translator's note*.] came lumbering over Lechfeld. She became the target for my first practice jet-fighter attack. I knew that I had been put into the air more for a technical opinion than a tactical one and that my man-oeuvres would be viewed with some disquiet from the ground. Raw eggs were handled with less circumspection than these products of a hybrid technology. But already I knew that what these aircraft promised surpassed all previous notions and ideas to such an extent that whatever uncertainties might still remain could be utterly disregarded.

After landing I was impressed and inspired as never before. What was decisive was proven capability and character. This was a great leap forward!

We drove back to the factory for a closing discussion. There behind us on the apron, glinting silver in the sunshine of this May day, stood the Me 262. And it was like 'a ray of silver on the horizon' in the figurative sense too.

Today I remain convinced that my optimism was not misplaced in expecting that the deployment *en masse* of the Me 262 would have brought about a fundamental change in German air defence. My only fear was that the enemy would catch up or even beat us to it. This worry was one of the few which were unfounded. The deployment of the Me 262 *en masse* failed to take place for other reasons. I could not have anticipated those reasons as, immediately after my first test flight, I sent the following telex to Feldmarschall Milch:

'The Me 262 aircraft represents an enormous leap which secures for us operationally an unimaginable advantage if the enemy continues with piston drive. In the air the machine makes a very good impression. The engines are completely convincing except at take-off and landing. The aircraft opens up fully new tactical possibilities.'

Shortly before Galland's arrival, Späte had also experienced a fire when starting up. Perhaps he had moved a thrust lever injudiciously. After the Me 262 flights by Opitz and Galland in May 1943, Milch changed his opinion about the jet and at a conference in Berlin on 2 June he agreed to run an Me 262-0 pilot series 'because of its superior speed as well as its many other qualities'. When Milch announced that fighter manufacture would be increased to 4,000 machines per month, Galland pleaded for a production ratio of 3,000 conventional Fw 190 and 1,000 Me 262, extra capacity for the jet being created by rejecting the less promising Me 209. Milch stated that he could not approve developing the jet in such numbers at the expense of conventional fighters because 'the Führer considers the risk to be too great'. Personally he would heartily welcome a planned series production of such magnitude but as a soldier he had no option but to follow orders and 'if the Führer orders caution, we must be cautious'.

A few days after this meeting Hitler watched an Me 262 exhibition flight and saw the aircraft's impressive qualities for himself. On 27 August 1943 the Ministry contracts division ordered Messerschmitt AG to set up the Me 262 in series production.

Substantial delays occurred in the execution of the order. On 17 August, USAAF bombers had attacked the Messerschmitt works at Regensburg. The factories were severely damaged and the valuable rigs for the Me 262 fuselages destroyed. Junkers had advised that the Jumo turbojet 004, 109–004B of 900 kilos thrust, would not be ready for fitting in the engine nacelles until October. Finally there were concerns about the known weaknesses of the Messerschmitt AG management – the works had already found itself in difficulties over smaller contracts and with its inadequate structure might fail altogether with a major order. In this regard senior officials at the Reich Air Ministry were aware that Professor Messerschmitt often made promises about developments and delivery schedules which he was subsequently unable to keep. This would ultimately prove to be the case with the Me 262.

On 2 November 1943 Hitler involved himself directly in Me 262 production by sending Goering in person to Augsburg to find out from Messerschmitt whether the aircraft could be fitted out as a bomber. In response to the Reichsmarschall's question, Messerschmitt stated categorically that the original plans contained bomb retention and release gear for two bombs of 250 kg or one of 500 kg. Goering – surprised by Messerschmitt's welcome answer – responded by saying that the Führer had only mentioned two bombs of between 50 kg and 100 kg, but it would be so much the better if the Me 262 could carry two bombs of 250 kg or one of 500 kg. In conclusion he enquired when the machines of this type would be available.

The question embarrassed Messerschmitt. He was anxious to avoid provoking a controversy during Goering's visit but a mealy-mouthed answer would not now avail him and he was forced to resort to the truth. The fact of the matter was, he said, that the bomb gear had not actually been developed yet, adding hastily that there would be no special difficulty fitting it to the test aircraft immediately after the device had been manufactured. Annoyed at this sudden change in the situation, Goering retorted, 'You said that the aircraft was to be fitted with the bomb gear from the beginning!'

Messerschmitt struggled vainly to extricate himself by re-phrasing his original statement. What he had meant to say was that all accessories had been provided for in the production plans, he said. The now sceptical Reichsmarschall demanded an unequivocal answer to his question exactly what the delay would be. Messerschmitt made the unconvincing response: 'Oh, not very long. Perhaps two weeks. It's not a big problem, we still have to make a sort of cover for the bomb claw.'

Here was the conflict: the machine was entering series production as a fighter bomber, i.e., based on original plans containing bomb retention and release gear. This gear was not available although Messerschmitt had implied that it was. Goering received another shock when he learned that not a single model from the pilot series was available for test flight as a bomber. There were only two original prototypes still extant, Messerschmitt said: one of the first three had been destroyed in a crash and the other two were both badly damaged. From this moment on, Goering realised that the production management team at Messerschmitt AG needed to be closely monitored and accordingly he appointed Oberst Petersen, head of the Rechlin Test Centre, to form a commission which would have responsibility for Me 262 development.

On 12 November 1943 Milch asked the Technical Office Chief of Staff, General Vorwald, for his opinion of the Me 262:

> The only doubt we still have is the question of whether the turbojets have been tested sufficiently so that we can go into full production in the coming year. What is your opinion on that?

Vorwald expressed no doubts himself but Major Knemeyer of the Rechlin Test Centre warned of the catastrophic situation at Messerschmitt AG 'where everything had run into a bottleneck'. His opinion was based on a bitter complaint by the Chief of Procurement and Supply about the worrying extensions to agreed production periods and the juggling with figures, statistics and delivery dates by the Company.

Since his first jet flight, six months had passed during which time General der Jagdflieger Adolf Galland had spared no effort attempting to have the Me 262 fighter scheduled for series production. He considered it highly favourable therefore when Goering arranged to present Hitler with an exhibition of the latest aircraft and weapons at Insterburg in East Prussia on 26 November 1943. With a great hoo-ha and in the presence of a great host of high officials, officers and NSDAP (*Nationalsozialistische Deutsche Arbeiterpartei*, the National Socialist German Workers' Party) people, the Reichsmarschall appointed himself – and not without the odd *faux pas* – master of ceremonies.

When the assembly arrived at the Me 262 aircraft and Goering had ended his introduction, Hitler asked suddenly, 'Can this aircraft also carry bombs?' As to the response there are various accounts.

David Irving wrote in his book *Die Tragödie der Luftwaffe*:

> Hitler repeated his question if this fighter could also carry bombs. Before the others could stop him, Messerschmitt stepped forward and said, 'Jawohl, mein Führer, it can take a 1000-kg or two 500-kg bombs without a problem.' Hitler thanked him: 'This is finally the Blitzbomber, this is finally the aircraft, that I have been asking the Luftwaffe to provide for years. Here it is, and only one man has recognised it!'[1]

A slightly different version appears in General Galland's book *Die Ersten und die Letzten*:

> ...the Me 262 jet fighter attracted special attention. I was standing close to Hitler when he surprised Goering with the question: 'Can this aircraft carry bombs?' Goering had already discussed the matter with Messerschmitt and left it to the Professor to answer: 'Jawohl, mein Führer, in principle yes. As regards a 500-kg payload certainly, maybe even 1000-kg if strengthened.'

Galland commented:

> It was a carefully formulated and straightforward response to which one could hardly object. Among airmen this answer would have raised no eyebrows. For every expert knew that it was purely hypothetical. The Me 262 was not equipped with retaining or release gear for bombs, nor fusing installation, nor bombsights. Its flight characteristics and the panorama from the cockpit made it unsuitable for aimed bombing. The only possible bombing tactic was some sort of dive, but this would have involved the aircraft exceeding its permitted maximum speed. Above 950 kph the aircraft was no longer controllable. At low altitude the fuel consumption was so great that no useful penetration over enemy territory was possible, therefore low-flying attacks did not enter into it. All that actually remained was horizontal bombing from altitude.

However, under the given circumstances the target needed to be the size of a large town to be certain of obtaining a hit.

But who would have wanted to offer a dissertation of this kind to Hitler at such a moment? How would one know that the argument had even been understood, let alone accepted? I admit that the Reichsmarschall, with whom Hitler had been speaking previously, might have had the duty to make him aware of all this. If he actually did do so I have no idea. In any case, Hitler allowed Messerschmitt and the rest of us no opportunity for explanations but continued, 'For years I have been asking the Luftwaffe for the fast bomber which, whatever the enemy fighter defences, is certain to reach its target. In this aircraft, which you tell me is a fighter, I see the Blitzbomber with which I will repulse the invasion in its initial and weakest phase. Ignoring the enemy air umbrella it will strike into the masses of material and troops which have just come ashore and sow panic, death and destruction. That is finally the Blitzbomber! And naturally, nobody has thought of it as such!'

A third account appears in copious file notes made by Professor Messerschmitt himself following a telephone conversation with his brother-in-law Professor Madelung in 1971. They were discussing David Irving's version (the notes in square parentheses clarifying Messerschmitt's remarks are the author's).

Messerschmitt: The 262 was not built to be a fighter. When Hitler asked me in East Prussia if the 262 could also carry bombs I said, 'Of course.' Firstly I fitted [probably he means here 'I was the first to fit'] bomb retention gear to a fighter [Me 109]. From the very beginning the 262 was always thought of as suitable for modification into a fighter bomber. During the Polish campaign I had the idea of hanging a couple of bombs [to the Me 109] and went with Voigt [Chief of Projects Office] to Berlin and visited Udet, who was then chief of the Technical Office, Lucht [General Staff Engineer at the Reich Air Ministry] and Reichenbach [General-Engineer in charge

of Development at the Ministry of Aircraft Production].
When I suggested what I had in mind they thought I was
joking. On the way home I said to Voigt, 'We will just make a
little something, it won't cost much and we'll hang a 50-kg
bomb below an Me 109.' We did it and a few weeks later tried
it out and it was a complete success. Then we rang Berlin and
said we wanted to demonstrate it. Suddenly we got the
contract to fit bombs to all Me 109s. With the 262 we
envisaged it from the very beginning, it was included in the
design sketches. I thought of putting the bombs in front of
the retraction mechanism [the undercarriage shaft] for the
wheels a little forward of the centre of gravity.

Madelung: Where was Hitler's error?

Messerschmitt: I don't know. It was purely an operational
question. I didn't convert the machine and if anyone says I did
that is a distortion and a lie. Where the machines we built
went to I have no idea.

Madelung: Up to now it has always been said that Hitler prevented the proper use of the 262 because he ordered it to be
converted to a bomber.

Messerschmitt: One can't speak of conversion because the fighter
was planned as a fighter bomber from the outset. My 200 [Ha
200, a light fighter and trainer developed by Messerschmitt in
Spain after the war] and the 300 [Ha 300, a modern fighter aircraft developed by Messerschmitt in Spain, the prototypes of
which were sold by Franco to Nasser in Egypt; further work
was carried out on the type under Messerschmitt's super-
vision] were also designed as such.

This account by Professor Messerschmitt contains many true
statements but also errors and lapses of memory. That there were
early trials of the Me 109 as a fighter bomber is a fact. That the Me
262 could also have been used as such in the ground-attack role is
proved by the later addition of the R4M rockets beneath the wings
as is mentioned later. But in the opinion of all pilots and engineers
involved, the Me 262 was definitely never designed nor fitted to be
a bomber capable of carrying even a medium load. Messerschmitt's

response to Hitler that the 262 could carry a payload of between 500 kg and a tonne can only be understood as the claim of an industrialist scenting an additional order. That was his right, of course, for operational matters were never his business. Had Hitler perhaps posed the question in the form 'how long it would take to equip the Me 262 to carry a one-tonne bomb', Messerschmitt would have had to say at least a year. Seen from that perspective, the Me 262 would have been a different, almost a new aircraft. Building the prototype, testing the machine and the bomb gear and sights in flight and preparing it for operational readiness would have taken at least another twelve months after the conversion to a two-seater. Galland, Petersen and, of course, Goering knew that. It will remain an unsolved mystery why – with the exception of Milch – nobody attempted to make Hitler aware of the fact. As Luftwaffe Commander-in-Chief and Reichsmarschall it was unquestionably Goering's duty to do so, for there were no 'proper channels' for him to go through. But it is obvious that we have here an 'un-plugged hole' that cannot be explained away by the fear of Hitler's allergy to counter-argument respecting the Me 262 in the fast bomber role. Certainly if there had been an energetic resistance hats would have rolled if not heads. Yet twelve months later when the ineffective officers' revolt reported by Steinhoff and Galland took place it went unpunished. The bull must occasionally be taken by the horns and the admirable operations of Jagdverband 44 which followed the said 'revolt' were by far more dangerous to health than tackling Hitler respectfully about the Me 262.

The real guilty party was Goering. He had fallen from grace and lacked the courage to chance Hitler's now undisguised disfavour. He who barely eight months previously had refused Milch the use of fighter aircraft was now not only silent but – according to Irving – actually approved a variation of the jet-fighter project which meant a setback of months. Galland also kept a still tongue although at least he and his office were not inactive behind the scenes.

The Arado aircraft firm was turning out the Ar 234, a jet bomber not far behind the Me 262 in development. This would have been the right machine for Hitler's bomber idea, but the pressures of time, difficulties in obtaining materials and fuel, crew training, the deteriorating situations on the various fronts and – as before – Hitler's sensibilities, all combined to ensure that nothing came of it. In the event, in a telex dated 5 December 1943, Hitler ordered the Ar 234 to be used in the fast reconnaissance role for which it would be at operational readiness by the autumn of 1944. It was also turned out as a bomber designated Ar 234-B2, but this version did not make its appearance until the end of 1944. By the war's end only about 200 Ar 234 jets had been built and used operationally. Many went to training units, others to bomber squadron KG76 and some were probably used as stop-gaps in the fighter ranks.

Hearing Messerschmitt's reply to Hitler's question regarding the possibility of making the Me 262 into the Blitzbomber, Oberst Petersen of the Rechlin Test Centre remarked in an undertone to his neighbour, 'That's torn it!', and he was proved right.

Hitler, whom nobody in his entourage dared contradict, remained adamant that the Me 262 must be used as a fast bomber. Whatever difficulties and objections there might be did not interest him. He had, after all, solved more awkward problems. Aside from the weapons of reprisal, he had nothing more to add on the subject of the appalling and ever increasing bombardment of Germany's cities and industry.

Thousands of tons of explosives rained down on Germany day and night. In the week when German fighters shot down 300 enemy bombers, the enemy took note of this fact and exacted revenge by destroying 700 Me 109s on the production line, to-gether with large areas of the various assembly works. But the Me 262, which as the only superfast fighter in the world could have brought to a halt these lethal depredations, was not available. There was evidence that the Allies could not continue to operate over Reich air space at a 10 per cent loss rate in aircraft per raid. The first delivery of mass-produced Me 262 fighters was scheduled for May 1944. If this date had been kept, it would not have brought the turning of the tide overnight but it would – as would later be proved – have put a large dent in the air supremacy which the Allies enjoyed from the summer of 1944.

In this connection mention must be made of the Me 163 rocket fighter. This most modern fighter could also have been operational earlier if its final development stage to operational readiness had been given a higher priority from the beginning. Because of its very limited range the Me 163 escaped consideration for the Blitz-bomber role. The Walter rocket engine had tanks for two tonnes of fuel which lasted five minutes. The aircraft could reach ten kilometres altitude in ninety seconds or so. This was sufficient for a brief attack on any enemy formation sighted from the airfield. Speeds of 900 kph were obtained giving the Me 163 the same superiority as the Me 262 if only very temporarily. It was planned that operational Me 163 units would be dotted all along Germany's western border from the sea to Switzerland, from where they would shoot up to intercept incoming enemy bombers with their fighter escorts. It was not a bad plan so long as the weather held good. With a low overcast the practice would be for the pilot to abandon the aircraft after the attack and descend by parachute. In good visibility, conditions of high cloud or clear skies, the Me 163 had to glide back to the airfield once its fuel was spent. In a glide the Me 163 was at the mercy of any passing enemy aircraft as was the Me 262 when landing.

Consideration was given to using the Me 163 as a ram fighter but nothing ever came of the idea. The strength of the German fighter arm was entrusted to the Me 109 and its famed successor, Kurt Tank's Fw 190. The consequence of the visit by Milch and Udet to Augsburg in August 1941 had been a new aircraft production programme whereby the planned output of the Fw 190 exceeded by 250 per cent that of the Me 109.

5

The Me 262 as Bomber

The Crucial Lost Year

Tens of thousands of bombs fell on German cities and centres of industry in the six months between General Galland's first flight in the Me 262 jet and the Insterburg airfield exhibition of November 1943. The German people were exposed to a rain of fire which claimed its victims young and old without mercy. The neglected Reich air defences were poorly equipped to prevent it. Many former leading senior Luftwaffe command and fighter-arm officers maintain today that the deployment of the Me 262 could have reduced substantially the extent of the catastrophe, and not a few of them consider that it would have turned the tide. The jet fighter success in the last months of the war proved that the Me 262 might have brought the incessant flow of Allied bombers over the Reich largely to a halt.

Unceasing operational missions and a high casualty rate had made the air-war critical for both sides. Initially the Allies were short of fighter escorts and suffered almost intolerable losses on bomber operations. As time progressed it became clearer that the Luftwaffe was short of materials and fuel. Its ability to defend Reich air space was weakening, and this gave Allied fliers the hope that total air supremacy was just around the corner.

On the German side, fighter and bomber crews alike operated as a force hopelessly inferior in numbers and stretched to the limit by the excessive demands made upon them. Enemy bomber streams were becoming ever larger, fighter escorts faster and by virtue of longer ranges able to protect the bombers far deeper into Germany than hitherto. The Luftwaffe fleet of obsolete bombers and mainly obsolete charismatic fighters was simply no match for their opponents. They knew it and it affected their morale: only a flier who has experienced the sensation personally can know the sickening dread before a hopeless mission with the odds stacked against him.

To put it in a nutshell, there were too few pilots, too few machines, those machines in service were too slow and fuel was scarce. In the air Luftwaffe fighters had to chance the enormous field of defensive fire of the four-engined bombers, yet they knew the enemy's airborne radio and radar technology was superior. But despite it all a miracle happened and in these six months hundreds of enemy bombers were destroyed in raids on Berlin, Schweinfurt, Bremen, Münster and Marienburg.

Regarding the American losses alone Galland commented in *Die Ersten und die Letzten*:

> Of course, with the increase in squadron strengths the losses also rose. According to US statistics their bomber arm lost 727 aircraft over Europe in the first ten months of 1943…

This notable success was achieved by German fighter men operating under the severest combat conditions, and most of them were not flying the modern Fw 190 but the Me 109 and at night the slower Me 110 two-seater. It is difficult to estimate how much greater their success might have been if throughout they had had faster fighters with longer range, the Me 262 especially, which though present in smaller numbers was certain to have swelled Allied bomber losses. But the wrangling over the aircraft went on and on. By the time that Erprobungskommando 16 was testing the Me 163 rocket fighter operationally at Bad Zwischenahn near Oldenburg in July 1943, there was still no talk of series production let alone operations.

There was a number of reasons for this state of affairs. Hitler's trust in Goering had wavered. When the Reichsmarschall obtained an audience with Hitler, he no longer had his former influence. It was therefore not to be expected that Goering might achieve a higher priority for Me 262 series production. Probably the most telling blow against the aircraft, however, came from a most unexpected source, Willy Messerschmitt himself. In a conversation on 27 June 1943 at Obersalzberg with Hitler, Messerschmitt warned him of Milch's planning errors particularly with regard to the latter's ideas about future aircraft production and choice of types. He even went so far as to caution Hitler against mass-producing the Me 262 on the grounds of its enormous fuel consumption. It seems incomprehensible that he would have offered such advice but the fact is confirmed historically by two sources: Rakan Kokothaki, who was present when Messerschmitt reported back to his directors on his conversation next day, and David Irving (*Die Tragödie der Luftwaffe*, pp 294–5) quoting Kokothaki and the Soviet interrogation of Messerschmitt postwar.

After Messerschmitt's statement to the board, Hitler and Speer expressed doubts about making the Me 262 the mainstay of the German fighter arm. Actually there had never been talk of such a thing. What was being asked for was the addition of this superfast and superior machine to the Reich air defence force alongside the Fw 190 and the Me 109 as soon as possible. Neither Milch nor Galland nor anybody else from the Reich Air Ministry or Luftwaffe could have intended to make the Me 262 the mainstay of the fighter arm overnight. It would have been in any case many months ahead, for the opportunity simply would not have existed to re-train fighter squadrons for the new jet nor create the infrastructure for the aircraft at squadron level. The assertion about the fuel was correct so far as it went, but jet fuel is not costly kerosene but a type of diesel oil requiring less refining and so subject to less reduction in preparation.

Though not referring to it specifically, Rust and Hess argue cogently in their article 'The German Jets and the USAAF' (1963) that Messerschmitt's outburst of 27 June 1943 was undoubt-edly the turning point for the aircraft's future. Hitler's primary fear was that a lightly damaged Me 262 might make an emergency landing in enemy-held territory whereby the secrets of the aircraft's construction and its turbojets would be forfeited. It was not known in Germany at the time that the United States and Britain were only one year behind in the development of similar jet aeroplanes. When Hitler was informed what difficulties were to be expected from operational flying at low level, such as reduced speed, high fuel consumption, vulnerability to enemy fighters and so on, this would explain his decision that the Me 262 was not to be used as a fighter, they say. Unfortunately for the argument, the Me 262 fighter would not have run the risk of crashing on enemy-held territory if it had been operational over Berlin, for example.

Obviously there was some other reason why the aircraft was wanted in the bomber role. On 2 November 1943 Goering went to Augsburg to investigate whether the aircraft was suitable for use as a fighter bomber. Three weeks later at Insterburg Hitler enquired of Messerschmitt about the aircraft's bomb-carrying capability and he used the term 'Blitzbomber' specifically. Rust and Hess then continue:

> Hitler saw the Me 262 as a Blitzbomber. He did not realize that converting the Me 262 into an effective two-seater bomber aircraft with the necessary bomb-aiming apparatus and bomb-release gear, not to mention adequate range, involved completely redesigning the aircraft. A conversion of this kind would have put back the operational readiness of the Me 262 by many months – certainly beyond when the invasion was expected.

This assumption by Rust and Hess seems to go a little too far, for being informed of all the complaints about the Messerschmitt set-up and their causes, Hitler had Goering issue an order of the day on 5 December 1943 to the effect that:

> The Führer wishes to draw our attention urgently to the enormous importance of the production of jet aircraft to be deployed as fighter bombers. It is imperative to ensure that by the spring of 1944 the Luftwaffe has a sufficient number of these fighter bombers operational. Any difficulties caused by raw-material and manpower shortages are to be overcome by the transfer of Luftwaffe supplies and personnel so that

anything which might lead to a prolongation of the manu-facturing period is removed. The Führer makes it known that all delays in our jet-fighter programme will be tantamount to irresponsible negligence. The Führer requires that with effect from 15 November 1943 a written report is submitted to him every two months regarding the current progress on the Me 262 and Ar 234 programmes.

This order, though not the result of Goering's visit to Augsburg, signified the final classification of the Me 262 as a fighter bomber and not the pure fighter which Messerschmitt had constructed and which the German fighter arm needed so desperately. After the loss of North Africa, the end of the alliance with Italy and the shrinking perimeter of the various fronts, the most powerful weapons of attack were now necessary on land and in the air to defend against the enemy. One of these weapons would have been the Me 262 fighter.

The only plausible reason why Messerschmitt might want to protect himself against a full-scale production run of the Me 262, or at least to defer it, lay elsewhere.

The fantastic success of the Me 109 had made Willy Messer-schmitt into a celebrity worldwide. Its victories in 1939 and 1940 had endowed the machine with a kind of mystique. For its builder and his factory it brought almost a monopoly on fighter production confirmed semi-officially in a conversation between Udet and Ernst Heinkel reported in the latter's memoir *Stürmisches Leben*.

Heinkel, whose doubtlessly more efficient He 112 had been completed a little later than Messerschmitt's Bf 109, must have been bitterly disappointed to lose out when in 1936/1937 the Bf 109 was chosen for the standard German fighter. A year or so later Heinkel observed to Udet, with whom he was on the friendliest terms, 'The next fighter is Heinkel's!' Udet demurred. 'The official view now is that aircraft manufacturers should specialise in particular types. It is a rationalisation. On account of his success with the Bf 109, Messerschmitt will take over the fighters. And, after the He 111, you will develop only bombers. The Bf 109 will keep us going for at least four years. It will soon have the 1000-hp

Daimler–Benz engine. That will give it about 550 kph, and with the improved version, 600. Meanwhile Messerschmitt is working on a new twin-engined fighter. We have no more fighter problems…'

Nobody could then have anticipated how heavy a cross to bear this last sentence would later become. No wonder therefore that Messerschmitt might feel as though his back were to the wall when the Me 209 and Me 309, successors to the Me 109 in 1942 and 1943, both drew the short straw and lost him the battle for the series contract. And he lost it not only to Kurt Tank's better Fw 190, but also to his own Me 109G and the Me 262.

From the beginning of his career, Messerschmitt was known as an avid aircraft designer, an engineer whose inspirations gave him no rest. A fund of anecdotes depicts him in a coffee shop, on a train, in a car at traffic lights, fumbling through his pockets for a scrap of paper on which to scribble down a concept or draft a rough sketch. His staff had dozens of such stories to tell, but they also reported how the expenditure of capital for his work at Bamberg made his family nervous wrecks. After the move to Augsburg, under the partnership agreement with Bayerische Flugzeugwerke, the company's accounts office picked up the tab for his numerous wide-ranging projects. It was a trait of his character that Messerschmitt would generally find the way to offset personal financial risk. The Me 210 disaster for which he was personally responsible cost Messerschmitt AG at least RM 30 million, a sum which would be difficult to claw back even in an epoch when the company was buried under an avalanche of armaments contracts.

Messerschmitt saw it as his moral obligation to recoup this vast sum but he was imbued by now with a greater degree of caution. Whereas the Me 262 was an outstandingly advanced machine, how it would behave operationally once it was in series production was an unknown factor. Moreover as yet the jet engines were not fully reliable nor had the airframe been tested to the parameters: test speeds had been restricted to the normal limits of propeller aircraft.

It had been a similar story with regard to the Me 163 which – contrary to many assertions – was designed and built by Alexander Lippisch. By his own admission Messerschmitt never had a finger in the pie and treated the project with disinterest if not disdain. The Me 163 airframe had proven flawless in tests over the range of speeds of which it was capable. The rocket motor on the other hand had some diabolical traits and occasionally incinerated the pilot. As an Me 163 glided in to land it was at the mercy of any lurking enemy fighter, a problem which would be shared by the Me 262 on its landing approach. Additionally if an Me 262 engine had to be shut down the aircraft could fly home but no evasive manoeuvres were possible if attacked.

Piston-engined aircraft were not vulnerable in this way. These drawbacks could not be lightly glossed over, least of all by Messerschmitt. Therefore preparation of the Me 262 for operations would not follow the same course as a typical propeller aircraft such as the Me 209 and 309 had done.

Unencumbered by problems of high finance, fighter men, their commanders and senior officers like Galland saw the situation more soberly and thus in a truer light. By 1943 they could probably have proved that the Luftwaffe was likely to lose out entirely to the endless stream of enemy bombers if Reich air defences were not strengthened significantly very soon. Many eye-witness accounts of the time, letters, file notes and diary entries, provide a confusing and grotesque picture of the altercations at Luftwaffe High Command and in the General Staff which by-passed Goering and went directly to Hitler. The Reichsmarschall of the very battered German Reich was already its saddest figure.

He had finished the World War I as a fighter pilot with an impressive twenty-two kills. He had taken command of the famous Richthofen fighter squadron (although not to the universal acclaim of its officers). A member of the NSDAP from 1922, he was one of Hitler's 'Old Guard', became the most senior SA-chief and was seriously wounded in that role during the march to the Feldherrnhalle on 9 November 1923. As the 'true Paladin of the Führer' he became Prussian Minister–President after the National Socialist seizure of power in 1933, Prussian Interior Minister, the Reich Minister for Aviation, the Reich Minister for Forestry and Hunting and finally Commander-in-Chief of the Luftwaffe.

It is clear that this vain and occasionally drug-dependent man never fulfilled his true potential. His staff, fighter men and officers who knew him or had conversations with him often spoke highly of his intelligence and good judgment. Nobody took amiss his extrovert personality, his fantasy uniforms, the theatrical arrivals, the extravagance of his title with the prefix '*Reichs-*'. They smiled and accepted him as he was. Among the people he was even loved, for he brought something of a monarchic flair to the otherwise spartan customs of Adolf Hitler. He had insisted that he be called '*Maier*' – peasant farmer – if so much as one solitary bomb fell on German soil, but even when the air-raid sirens howled incessantly the people were not aggrieved at Goering. They simply called him *Maier* and left it at that.

With all these quirks of character and his poor grasp of technical matters Goering was unfit to command the Luftwaffe. Understandably, and probably knowing this, the job of ensuring that he retained office became his main preoccupation. Assuredly he knew that it was at Hitler's whim that he stood or fell, and so he kow-towed and stayed in office. He was not an evil man: rather he may be compared to a pastor unversed in the Bible. Possibly that may be an important reason for his failure to argue the Me 262 to Hitler. By his sworn oath and without regard to whether it might lose him his office – supported mainly by Milch, Galland, Petersen, Gollob but also others – he was duty-bound to make known to Hitler his personal opinion and that of his technical experts. In the end he came up with a way to avoid biting the bullet by delegating his responsibility. There was a man who had been demanding a fast and effective bomber for years. And that man was General der Kampfflieger, Oberst Dietrich Peltz.

Peltz had been learning his trade since Udet advocated the dive-bomber and converted the Immelmann fighter squadron into a Stuka unit. The obvious problem from the outset was aiming at and hitting the target. World War I had provided little useful experience, for the leap of technology in the intervening years was too great. The premature outbreak of war in 1939 had interfered with experiments to establish a reliable method and then train the crews. Naval air units flying the He 60 over the Hela Peninsula during the Polish campaign carried two 25-kg bombs in the cockpit and tossed them out over the target, aiming by eye. Moreover the Luftwaffe was still considered as a kind of extended arm of the other two services and not as an arm of service with its own strategic objectives. The air-war which developed after 1939 was foreseen only by a few visionaries.

In the first years of Hitler's war, it was Peltz who developed a viable dive-bombing procedure in which the flight leader went in ahead while the remainder of his formation circled nearby. After he had bombed he told them by radio how to approach the target. On account of the more reliable weather this method was taught at Foggia in Italy during the summer of 1942 using the reflecting gun-sight. Somewhat later the firm of Zeiss came to Foggia with the new and more reliable BAZ-bombsight resembling a small computer which provided the aiming point from data including the angle of dive, airspeed, air pressure, wind strength and other factors.

Many difficulties were ironed out or at least reduced in training flights and by using filmed simulations. These exercises with the Ju 88 were followed by operations in Norway, North Africa and over England led by Peltz. It was mainly here that he accumulated the vast experience which caused him to view the planned deployment of the Me 262 as a fighter bomber or Blitzbomber with extreme scepticism.

In the summer of 1943 in the rank of Oberst he had been appointed General der Kampfflieger. With it he inherited a measure of responsibility for the future of the Me 262. The call for faster bombers was justified and there had been improvements. But bombsights were complicated instruments and nobody on operations knew that better than Dietrich Peltz. Shortly after his appointment he was summoned to Goering's presence to render an account of his deliberations regarding the fitting-out of bomber squadrons with the Me 262 Blitzbomber. Peltz informed his commander-in-chief frankly of all the impediments identified to date and which had not been resolved. How was the target to be hit? What would the pilot aim with? In what manner would the one or two bombs be dropped? The Me 262 could not be dived! Bombing in level flight it would need luck to hit a field over a square kilometre in size. Pinpoint bombing was out of the question. Even if the two bombs had a shrapnel effect their effectiveness would still depend on luck. 'Bearing all this in mind,' he told Goering, 'if you ask me if the Me 262 can be a bomber Yes or No, I would say No! At least, not without thorough preparation and – probably – completely new bombsights.'

Anticipating Hitler's anger if he delivered such a depressing opinion, Goering was unrestrained: 'I didn't make you General of the Bomber Arm so that you can tell me it won't work! You know very well that it is the Führer's wish to use the Me 262 as a bomber and it's your job to come up with something. So there!'

Peltz responded with still more reasons. 'In bad weather we cannot keep Me 262 formations together. If we are flying blind, we cannot simply group up over a radio beacon and attack in formation. Individual aircraft will have to operate alone and attack alone, or at least in small flights, and that will ruin their effectiveness.' Goering understood all this and took the point that Peltz was making. But Goering was no longer the man to tell Hitler that his plans for the Me 262 Blitzbomber wouldn't wash, and perhaps Goering never had been. In conclusion Peltz suggested that the jet be used as an interceptor 'to plug the leaky roof above Germany', but Goering was not listening. From his weakened position he would only stir Hitler to anger preaching Peltz' unassailable argument. His logical course of action in such a case was to abdicate his 'throne', but obviously the time was inopportune.

Peltz knew that nothing was required by the bomber squadrons more urgently than a fast bomber with the speed of an Me 262 but also diveable, equipped with a modern bombsight and endowed with long range. What he had been offered was a makeshift. Although fast, the Me 262 was never cut out to do any serious bombing. Even converted into an almost new type it would still not be useful in that role.

In mid-1943 every fourth to sixth Allied bomber either returned to base badly damaged or was lost over Germany. There is evidence that the US, and especially the RAF, bomber crews became so demoralised after the bloodletting over Schweinfurt, Hamburg, Berlin and other cities that they needed to be specially motivated for each fresh mission. This bore similarity to the situation in the

German fighter arm, whose statistics were equally grisly, a large proportion of their casualties being sustained in the hail of fire from a bomber's rear-guns. It was in the summer of 1943, when knowledge about the Me 163 rocket aircraft became widely known in fighter circles, that rumours also began to circulate about a jet coming into readiness. Nothing further was known. I was myself then attending the JG300 *Wilde Sau* Night-fighter School at Alten-kirchen in Thuringia. The training was hard and claimed its victims. Almost every night one or other of us failed to return. And that was in training, as pupils. There were not a few Knight's Cross holders among them who wanted to take an intensive course in blind flying and then dived blindly to their deaths. All were volunteers. The young ones came from fighter schools, the older ones from operational units on all fronts.

In July 1943 I was asked if I fancied flying the new rocket. I said 'Yes' without a moment's hesitation and three weeks later reported to Erprobungskommando 16 at Bad Zwischenahn. Our aircraft was the Me 163. The rocket. Including the commander and flight instructors there were some thirty pilots, mostly boys still wet behind the ears with little or no operational experience. Two instructors and one pupil had the Knight's Cross. The youngest of the three was killed the first or second time out. We received an introductory lecture about the dangers of rocket flight and were then offered the chance to return to the units from which we came. Only one man of the thirty stepped forward to accept the offer. The others remained even though we all now knew that a rocket could explode in flight. And not only in flight, but on the ground as well. On one occasion we put the human remains of a dead pilot – half a thigh – into a coffin… and carried on flying. This was how the morale of German fighter pilots, doubted by Goering, looked in those days. Yes, we were frightened. Again and again the fear came, crept up upon us in the night as we slept. But it disappeared once we took off.

Almost a year since Galland had flown the Me 262 for the first time in May 1943 and had recommended its operational use at the earliest opportunity, Hitler remained obstinate that the aircraft was a bomber. A whole year had been wasted, a whole year in which something tangible might have been done to counteract enemy air superiority effectively. How bitterly serious this situation proved in the train of this lost year was portrayed by Galland at an armaments conference in April 1944. In his book *Die Ersten und die Letzten* (pp 354–5) he wrote:

The problem the Americans set the German fighter arm – I am only speaking here of our fighters – is simply one of air superiority alone. This has now progressed to the stage where it verges on air supremacy. The adverse ratio in aircraft by day is between 1:6 to 1:8 approximately. The standard of the enemy's training is extraordinarily high. The technical standard of his aircraft is so notable that we have to say, something must happen soon!

The night-fighter arm has lost more than one thousand aircrew over the last four months. Among them was a number of the best flight leaders, group commanders and squadron commodores. It is very difficult to plug the gaps, not with numbers but with experienced pilots. In various addresses and reports I have spoken of the latest possibility: the danger of the collapse of the Luftwaffe! It has come to this because the enemy's numerical superiority has reached the stage where one has to say that the struggle is becoming extraordinarily unproductive for us.

What path should we take to get out of this situation? First we must rectify the adverse ratio: that is, industry must turn out a guaranteed number of aircraft to enable us to rebuild the fighter arm. Secondly, because we are numerically inferior and will always remain so – of that fact we are perfectly certain – we must increase the technical standard. I hold the point of view that already with a small number of technically high-value aircraft such as the Me 262 and Me 163 we can achieve an enormous amount. This polemic between fighter men – which aircraft is best to bring down enemy bombers by day – is to a large extent also a question of morale. The enemy's morale must be broken. With the help of the two components, numbers and technical advance, the fighting value of our squadrons and in retrospect the training standard are bound to be enhanced. I do not expect that we will ever manage to get on equal terms, but I do expect us to reach a reasonable ratio. In the last ten attacks we lost on average over fifty aircraft and forty pilots. This corresponds to five hundred aircraft and four hundred pilots in ten great raids. At such a tempo we cannot remedy a shortfall of such magnitude with the present standard of training.

I renew my plea that allied to an extraordinary effort to make up the aircraft numbers, the attempt will be made with the greatest energy to ensure that our technical advance is at least on a par. We must have such standards that the fighter arm regains the sensation of superiority even if their numbers are still less. And now as an example I state a value: at this moment I would prefer one Me 262 to five Me 109s…

This statement made the situation abundantly clear. One assumes that Hitler heard nothing of it and if it came to Goering's attention he took no notice of it. Yet it signalled uniquely the departure from grace of the Me 109 which had outlived its usefulness in the struggle against its competitors and the enemy. Even Willy Messerschmitt seemed to have recognised the folly of his statement to Hitler in June 1943. According to Galland, from now on Messerschmitt argued for the deployment of the Me 262 as an operational fighter aircraft but, in common with Milch and Galland, his pleas fell on deaf ears.

6

'Mein Führer, every child can see that that is a fighter and not a bomber!'

Oberst Edgar Petersen, former head of the central flight testing base at Rechlin, told me in 1976 that he still considered Messerschmitt's impetuous and ill-advised statement to Hitler at Insterburg that the Me 262 could carry a 1,000-kg bomb to be a turning point in the air-war. From the point of view of what payload the aircraft could carry Messerschmitt was, of course, right, but as a conscientious aircraft builder he ought to have qualified his remark by mentioning the time-factor involved in converting the Me 262 into a useful bomber.

Petersen remained convinced that to carry a heavy bombload the jet would have needed the more powerful Jumo 004C turbine, and these were still on the Junkers test-rig. Oberst Siegfried Knemeyer, a talented engineer on Goering's staff, gave the Me 262 a sporting chance as a fighter bomber, but with no more than two 50-kg bombs. Along with Galland, Milch, Gollob and others, General-leutnant Josef Kammhuber, one of the most successful organisers of the night-fighter arm, believed that if the machine had been used only in the fighter role round the clock, the civilian population would have been spared the more devastating raids.

One of the main reasons for Hitler's obstinacy was certainly the imminent invasion of northern France. The man who once had only waited for the opportune moment to land his troops in southern England was now haunted by the spectre of the invasion of Germany, something which he may have suspected that in the long run he was powerless to prevent, and he knew that it would betoken the end of all his great aims. On several occasions during his rise he had staked all upon a single card and won. Perhaps he saw the Me 262 fast bomber as his last ace.

Despite Hitler's order to produce the Me 262 as a bomber, the Messerschmitt works turned out the fighter version and one bomber variant. In the week of 20–25 February 1944 the Augsburg factory was almost totally gutted in a bombing raid and the pilot production was lost. After the fearful bombing raids of January and February 1944 Hitler ordered that the output of fighter aircraft must be increased to the maximum possible. At the same time he approved the highest priority for the so-called 'Jägernot Programm' – the emergency fighter programme launched on 1 March 1944 aimed at a greatly increased output of fighter aircraft in underground factories. In addition to existing production centres above ground, protected plants for the Me 262 were set up at Budweis in Bavaria, Neuburg/Donau in Austria and the REIMAHG (the REIchsMArschall Hermann Goering enterprise) underground installation near Grosseutersdorf, south of Jena, also known as Kahla, on the thickly afforested Walpersberg mountain. This was being developed into the main aircraft production centre for the Luftwaffe. Run by the SS using concentration-camp labour, it was already turning out an estimated 50 aircraft per day from its warren of internal tunnels when it was overrun in April 1945. A 1,000-yard airstrip ran the length of the mountain top. Completed aircraft were hoisted to the summit by a steep cable railroad and flown off to their operational squadrons.

Raging at the impotence of the Reich air defences to prevent them, Hitler had taken to heart the murderous air attacks of 'Big Week' which in February 1944 had paralysed the greater part of fighter-aircraft production and wrecked 700 Me 109s. But on the Me 262 he would not relent. A further serious blow to jet-fighter production was struck on 24 April 1944 when the Leipheim factory was also destroyed.

Hitler allowed no opportunity to pass, particularly at conferences, to enquire about how 'the Ar 234 and Me 262 jet bombers' were coming along. He would allow nothing to obstruct or influence or deflect him from that chosen path of which his highly valued aircraft builder had assured him, the suitability of the Me 262 for bomber duty.

Meanwhile, mainly at the instigation of Galland and Milch, and without the knowledge of Hitler and Goering, series production of the Me 262 fighter had begun. It was actually no more than a pilot run, twenty aircraft whose completion was reported in May 1944. Two of these twenty aircraft were damaged at the end of the delivery flight when the undercarriage collapsed on landing, one of the ferry pilots being killed. About the same time, work had begun on the fast bomber variant which – as predicted – was attended by so many difficulties and setbacks that fifteen to twenty months would be needed before its first prototypes were completed, thus approaching New Year 1946, by when Hitler's war had been long over.[2]

Galland and Milch did everything possible to follow up the pilot series by putting the Me 262 into mass production as a postulated fighter bomber with a retaining lock for lightweight bombs.

All that Galland had achieved so far with his persistent flow of recommendations and suggestions to Hitler was permission to set up a small test unit – Erprobungskommando 262 – at Lechfeld. Hitler had allowed this so that – as the Führer himself expressed it – the highly deserving General der Jagdflieger should receive a 'trinket'.

Erprobungskommando 262 Thierfelder – named for Haupt-mann Thierfelder its commander – had been formed in a very modest way at Lechfeld at the beginning of 1944. To set up the unit with the necessary machinery, tools and equipment was a long drawn-out business. No less difficult was the job of getting aircraft mechanics and transferring them in. The search extended into every nook and cranny at every air base. Lechfeld was a big airfield and Thierfelder's Kommando was only one of many. Outsiders raised no eyebrows at the strange aircraft seen there. The existence of the Me 262 jet had, of course, been common knowledge around Lechfeld for several years, although maybe the eyes of a few new arrivals widened in surprise when they first heard and saw it.

The new unit often drove Thierfelder to despair. He was an officer who through years of operational experience was accustomed to good order, clear instructions and a functioning organisation. This Kommando was a unique nightmare. Apart from the engineering people, ground staff and administration personnel he had only a personal Staff of three officers: Oberleutnants Wörner, an experienced fighter pilot as flight instructor, Rassmussen, his engineer officer, and Viktor Emanuel Preusker. As communications officer the latter had the difficult task of working out a reliable radio direction system for the Me 262, an extremely fast aircraft with limited range.

It was quite some time before the few Me 262s diverted from the bomber production line as a sop to Galland with Hitler's blessing made their appearance. In March 1944 Major Kogler, commander of III/ZG26 received orders to transfer two flights – Squadrons 8 and 9 with six pilots and part of the Squadron Staff – to southern Germany for Me 262 conversion training. The remainder of ZG26 had arrived in Germany shortly before to help stiffen the Reich air defence after previous service in North Africa and Italy. The engineers of 8th Squadron went to Leipheim, of 9th to Schwäbisch Hall, which were at the time the two final assembly workshops for the Me 262. The engineers were to learn how the aircraft was built and later take possession of the handful allotted. The six III/ZG26 pilots for conversion training at Lechfeld were Oberleutnants Bley, Müller-Nahlbach, Weber and Wegmann, Leutnant Schreiber and Feldwebel Lennartz. All were experienced Me 110 pilots. In April and May 1944 a number of young pilots without combat experience were drafted to Lechfeld for jet training.

Unexpected breakdowns and surprises cropped up in the conversion courses, primarily among the youngest pilots and those with little or no combat experience. The manipulation of the throttle lever was the major pitfall. From previous flying experience sitting behind a piston engine it was known that there had been no restrictions on moving the gas lever. Coming in to land too fast or too high one throttled back and went round for another try. To adjust position in formation you corrected by giving more or less gas. In practice, when dog-fighting you alternated between full throttle and feathering the motor as suited the situation. The Otto piston engines were always obliging, and if sometimes the engine choked on it, that was mostly harmless – a few splutters and then it burst back into life. But if you were anything robust about the way you pushed forward the throttle levers of the Me 262 jet turbines, they cut out and probably caught fire. Taking off, in the air, when landing. They caught fire if the throttle was advanced too quickly because more fuel came into the chambers than the engine could handle. It stopped the drive and the excess fuel then burnt off. If that happened before take-off, the airfield fire brigade or ground staff could quickly extinguish the fire once the jet was at a standstill. There would then be no further problem. At altitude an engine fire was dangerous, at low level usually fatal. At the outset of training especially it was a frequent occurrence, because pilots failed to observe the operating instructions from habit, inattentiveness or reacting in panic to an emergency.

A second but yet more deadly danger awaited the unwary in the steeper dives. It was the death of even good pilots who dived too fast. From level flight at perhaps 700 to 800 kph the speed of the Me 262 increased in seconds to 900 kph or more when put into a steep dive. It was not possible to recover the aircraft from such a dive using the original control stick of normal proportions. The muscular strength of the arms was insufficient to overcome the aerodynamic forces over the control surfaces. There were cases reported where pilots threw off the cabin hood and found that this had the effect of bringing the aircraft to tail-heavy, enabling control to be regained. If it happened – rarely at first – that in a dive the ailerons set themselves to nose-heavy, the pilot's only hope was the parachute, providing he had the altitude and experience. Three or four pilots lost on the earlier conversion courses at Lechfeld crashed for this reason, the cause initially causing perplexity.

Many accidents were due to the inexperience or nervousness of young pilots, but even for pilots with thousands of hours flying and front experience the Me 262 was the last aircraft they ever flew. Here in the majority of cases unexpected emergency situations or incorrect reactions in combat were the cause. On 12 May 1944 the synthetic fuel plants at Leuna and Politz were extensively damaged in USAAF air raids. This was the first dangerous hack at the Achilles' heel of the German Reich and Hitler realised that more such attacks would deprive him of an effective mechanised defence. A hectic programme of conferences was now begun at the highest level. The planned production of bomber and fighter aircraft was gone over repeatedly and reams of statistics produced. The possibility of its realisation changed from one day to the next. Goering, still in the dark about the true situation and what was possible, pleaded for a strong fighter arm and a no less strong bomber output. He studiously avoided taking the bull by the horns to disabuse Hitler of the notion that the invasion could be stopped by a notional 'fastest bomber'. Being little more than Hitler's lapdog, no doubt he felt his own powerlessness.

That was how matters stood when a decisive conference was fixed for 23 May 1944, held in the SS barracks at Obersalzberg on the slope below Hitler's residence. Goering had invited twenty representatives of the aviation and armaments ministries, of research, industry and the Luftwaffe including Reich Minister Speer, Milch, von Richthofen, Galland, Saur, Petersen (head of the Rechlin aircraft test base), Karl Frydag deputising for the managing director of Heinkel, Knemeyer and others.

Goering opened proceedings by delivering a potted history of mistakes of the past including a sly dig at the posthumous Udet, and rounded off with the by now customary exhortation substantially to strengthen the Luftwaffe in order to regain its former aerial superiority and above all to fend off the threatened invasion of the European mainland. Goering praised Udet for his Stuka idea and for carrying it through but then blamed him for neglecting bomber production to do so. Valuable time had been squandered on useless experiments to turn the giant He 177 into a dive bomber which had naturally gone awry. Goering placed special value on strengthening the day- and night-fighter arms. It had now become very urgent to combat the Allied bomber fleets over the Reich and bring to a halt the destruction of German cities and armaments factories. Hitler was expecting above everything an enhanced production of heavy bombers, especially the four-engined He 277 to which preference was being given and of which the Führer was demanding a future monthly output of at least 200 machines. Next in line came the Ju 287 which had already shown great promise in test flights. The lighter bombers Do 355 and Ju 388 would be used on the Western Front as fast bombers. Goering referred to the Ar 234 and Me 262 as 'support fighter bombers'. There was no more talk of the Me 262 as the 'fastest bomber', thus depriving those present of the chance to toss this subject into debate. Since Insterburg the Me 262 was no longer mentioned or discussed in wider circles. After Goering had told the assembly at the beginning of the conference of the urgent need for an increase in the defensive punch of the Reich defences, and those present had been informed that the production of the Me 262 fighter had already begun, if in small numbers, it seemed that the problems surrounding the Me 262 and its operational use must have been resolved. Those who were familiar with the problems of the aircraft by reason of their office or as engineers knew only too well that the Me 262 fighter bomber was depending on new jet turbines while the conversion to the 'fastest bomber' with a heavier bomb payload would take considerable time. In this respect there could be no answer to the most pressing questions.

After the conference, Speer, Milch, Petersen, Generals Galland and Korten and a few others made for the Berghof to discuss with Hitler the Jägerstab-Programm aimed at strengthening the fighter arm. The great 30-room Alpine-style house was set on a ledge at 1,700 metres. At that time besides the tight security on the ground, air defence was provided, the Waffen-SS manning sixty flak guns sited on various favourable heights: 12 x 10.5-cm, 16 x 8.8-cm, 24 x 3.7-cm, 6 x 2-cm and 2 x 2-cm quadruples and a 646-strong smoke-making unit. The Führer's air-raid centre was 30 metres below the Goeringhügel rock. It was linked to the national system and had a wall-map with numerous electrical circuits which lit up to show current enemy air movements over the Reich. If aircraft approach-ed nearer than 100 kilometres to Berchtesgaden the air-raid alarm went off. Since the possibility of a paratroop drop was also considered a possibility, on the roof of the produce warehouse lower down an observation bunker had been erected from where aerials and a scissors-type artillery binocular could be extended.

Hitler greeted the party only fleetingly, apparently deep in thought. Finally he took a seat and with a tired movement of the hand invited his guests to do the same. With seeming disinterest he listened to the briefing about the Jägerstab conference, occasionally making a short observation. His gaze was fixed on the Hoher Göll mountain which could be seen through the extensive south-facing window of the study. As Minister of Aircraft Production, General-feldmarschall Milch then delivered in a calm and factual manner a report about fighter output and fighter units which Hitler had requested, and mentioned the twenty Me 262s. Suddenly Hitler lowered his gaze to Milch as if horrified and asked in a guttural undertone: 'I thought the Me 262 was being produced as a fast bomber? How many of the completed 262s can carry bombs?'

Milch replied, 'None, mein Führer. The Me 262 is being built exclusively as a fighter aircraft.' By way of explanation he added that the conversion of the fighter into a fast bomber could not be achieved overnight but would take some time. Additionally the prototypes would have to be tested in flight. Milch concluded with the observation that even then the Me 262 would not be able to carry a bombload in excess of 500 kg.

In great excitement Hitler responded, 'That is irrelevant – I am only asking for a 250 kg bomb! I ordered it without asking any-body's opinion and I never left anybody in any doubt that it is to be produced as a fighter bomber!' At that moment, Oberst Petersen saw Goering incline himself towards Hitler's armchair and say in an undertone, 'See how they obey your orders, mein Führer!' Now it was obvious how deeply rooted Hitler's demand had been, and the importance he vested in the Me 262 as a fast bomber. The aircraft seemed to represent the fulfilment of a desire, the means finally to force his enemies to their knees. He had believed in Messer-schmitt's assurance, had ordered that it become reality, he had the men now standing in his presence to carry it through and – could they have dared to defy his orders?

Petersen, who in common with most others at the conference had never been informed by Goering or Milch of this Hitler re-quirement, felt his mind reeling. He heard Saur reciting the individual weights for the Me 262 armour and weapons, adding that they exceeded 500 kg. Hitler hardly allowed him to finish before barking: 'This aircraft is so fast that it doesn't need armour or guns.

They can all be taken out!'[3]

With that he turned directly to Petersen and said 'Is that so or not?' Still dazed by events Petersen, who was sure that a long dissertation would be pointless if not dangerous, merely answered, 'Yes, that goes without saying.' Milch, despairing as never before, attempted to interest Hitler in other opinions, but Galland, holding forth on the theme that no more time remained for modifications, was shouted down so brusquely by the Führer that he relapsed into silence.

Milch resumed by explaining calmly to Hitler that to have the Me 262 as a successful two-seater bomber represented a substantial reconstruction for which time was simply too short. Hitler rode over him rough-shod and with such violence of tone that Milch lost his head and shouted back, 'Mein Führer, every child can see that that is not a bomber but a fighter!'

Following this outburst Hitler turned his back on Milch without re-plying. Petersen's neighbour leaned towards him and said, 'And that's shot him down in flames.' It was the most apt description of this tragic collision of wills. A door had closed and would not re-open. Nobody knew this better than Milch who merely stood in silence as Hitler turned away from him. At this juncture Milch felt sure that he had reached the end of his career, but it did not depress him; whatever happened next, there was nothing he could do about it.

On 24 May 1944 a further conference was convened under Goering's chairmanship where the main topics were the Me 262 and Hitler's angry outbursts of the day before. Goering was as graceless as only he knew how to be even though the tone of the meeting was one of sober objectivity. From statements made by Petersen and Knemeyer, Goering and Milch learned for the first time that the 262 armour and guns had a total weight of about 600 kg, all of it forward of the aircraft's centre of gravity. It was therefore quite out of the question to do what Hitler had demanded and just jettison it to make way for a bomb of that weight slung below the fuselage. On the contrary, it would need an expensive modification to the whole design just to comply with this one order.

According to Irving, Goering raged: 'You gentlemen all seem to be deaf. I have repeated over and over the Führer's perfectly clear order that he doesn't give a hoot for the Me 262 as a fighter, he wants it exclusively as a fighter bomber… the Führer must have got a very peculiar idea about you. Everybody, Messerschmitt included, told him from the beginning that there is no doubt it can be done. Messerschmitt told the Führer in my presence at Insterburg, it was planned at the design stage that it can be made into a fighter bomber. Now suddenly it can't.'

Here Petersen interjected to rightly point out that the present engines were not suitable for bomber operations and required major modification. In view of the precarious situation the deployment of the Me 262 as a lightweight fighter was probably the best course although even then sacrifices would have to be reckoned with. A bomber variant was simply not on offer at the moment.

Goering's answer, again supplied by Irving: 'I would have been grateful if you had made ten per cent of these statements yesterday.' When Knemeyer confirmed Petersen's observations and also spoke out against a bomber variant, Goering interrupted him: 'The Führer says, as a fighter, as far as I'm concerned, you can burn it. What he needs is a bomber so fast that it can simply roar through the great mass of fighters which will be escorting the invasion force.' Goering now made a remark about the 'undisciplined load of military pigs' who had defrauded and deceived the Führer and himself. That he was the leader of these pigs was a point he appeared to have forgotten.

He now contented himself with the bitter reflection that after Messerschmitt's lightly given assurance at Insterburg, nobody had bothered to concern himself with what it involved, least of all Messerschmitt himself. It was primarily Messerschmitt's job to draft an opinion of what it entailed to fulfil Hitler's wish and set a time scale. Next down the line was Generalfeldmarschall Milch whose responsibility it had been to set it all out and at least advise his immediate superior, Goering, unequivocally about the technical situation. Milch had the competent men in his offices to do it. Both of them, Messerschmitt and Milch, had side-stepped their responsibility. It could only be explained by neither having taken Hitler's demand very seriously at the outset, or that they considered it a dangerous proposition to explain all the difficulties which Hitler was bound not to want to hear. Whatever the reason, the child was down the well and a precious year had been lost.

General Galland mentioned in his book *Die Ersten und die Letzten* another conference to which he was summoned together with Milch, Bodenschatz, Messerschmitt, Petersen and Saur. This was held on 29 May 1944, the date of Hitler's edict that the Me 262 and Ar 234 jets were to be built exclusively as bombers and not fighters. Goering informed the assembled officers that in order to avoid any misleading impressions in future the Me 262 was only to be spoken of as the 'Blitzbomber' and no longer as a fighter bomber. The meeting ended on a negative note. Messerschmitt – according to Galland – came out very strongly in support of the fighter generals and all gained the idea that Goering was not unimpressed by Galland's argument. But Goering was not willing to take it higher. At that level the subject was closed. After all that had gone before he knew what the reaction would be if he attempted to re-open it. With that, he took the Me 262 out of Galland's hands and gave it to Peltz.

It was at the end of May 1944 that all Me 262 development operations at Lechfeld, Leipheim, Schwäbisch Hall and other localities, with very few exceptions, were ordered to be suspended and the majority of pilots, most by now fully or semi-retrained for jets, were transferred out or returned to their former units to resume flying Me 109s and Fw 190s.

Günther Wegmann, one of the six III/ZG26 pilots, recalled the sense of shock and the mood of depression at the incomprehensible turn of events. It affected everybody and transformed their zeal into grim indifference. Pilots sat around in groups for hours mulling over the possible reasons for such an inconceivable instruction. Even the least experienced of them could imagine the hundreds of enemy fighters circling over the invasion force licking their chops as the Me 262 'fast bombers' arrived, the bombload hung below the fuselage depriving them of their priceless speed advantage. And those that escaped after dropping their bombs and survived the return flight to base could expect a worrying few minutes at their most vulnerable, sweeping in to land.

So began the last cruel act in the drama.

7

Kommando Nowotny –
The Sop to Galland

'We can carry out this operation on the English coast just the once while they are loading up on the beaches. After that, when they are unloading on the other side, between the landing craft and the beaches and against tanks just come ashore and so on. As I visualise it, the aircraft roar over the beaches and smash up all those heaps of material which are lying around in great confusion. That's how the Führer sees the operational use and that's how we are to prepare.'

Hermann Goering's words – quoted from Galland's book – referred to the Me 262 in the fast-bomber role acting against Allied invasion troops. In accordance with the will of the Führer, the Reichsmarschall had determined that the aircraft had no future as a fighter.

Galland, of course, was not prepared to take this lying down. The landing-craft notion was pure nonsense. Pilots and machines would be sacrificed without rhyme or reason. Scarcely a bomb would find its mark. Those dropped from a great height would all miss. The machine could not be used as a dive-bomber and at low level was easy meat for enemy fighters. That the latter would be present in large numbers to protect the landing craft was guaranteed. But the order had been given and presumably the disaster could no longer be averted.

The tremendous prospects for success which the Me 262 promised were demonstrated in the testing period by Thierfelder himself and the experienced former III/ZG26 pilots. The undisputed star was Leutnant Alfred Schreiber. Shortly after completing his conversion course he supplied the unequivocal proof for the efficacy of the jet aircraft in combat. In his first engagements he shot down five enemy aircraft one after the other, mostly RAF Mosquitos, the fastest enemy machine. He was summoned at once before a surprised Goering to make his report. If the Reichsmarschall conveyed notice of these successes with a covering memorandum, or whether they were mentioned in the daily situation conferences at Führer HQ, is not known, but apparently they influenced Goering's opinion strongly. Schreiber was later killed in action and is buried at Schwabstadl near Lechfeld.

Galland's staff included such proven fighting airmen as Gordon Gollob, Hannes Trautloft, Eduard Neumann and later Walther Dahl, and all now set to the task of making what they could of the Lechfeld successes. Nobody worried if a few intentional inaccuracies crept in. The end justified the means. Enemy fighter pilots captured after parachuting down from combat with an Me 262 were unanimous in confirming the absolute superiority of the German jet. Galland even came into possession of a report signed by General Spaatz, US Strategic Air Forces supreme commander, in which he spoke of 'the deadly German jet fighter'. The document was sent to Hitler with a covering memorandum.

Some of this propaganda may have borne fruit immediately after the Allied landings when, on 7 June 1944 in a conversation with Saur, Hitler modified his stance on the Blitzbomber question. While the initial production of the Me 262 had to remain limited to the bomber version, the testing of the fighter version by the Kommando at Lechfeld and the Rechlin Test Centre could continue so long as it did not interfere with bomber production. It was at this time that Hitler issued the order that operational Blitzbombers were forbidden to descend below 12,000 feet over enemy territory, an altitude at which, with no bombsight, they were next to useless as bomber aircraft.

Another method Galland used in the attempt to change Hitler's mind was to ask officers who were attending Führer HQ to receive awards from Hitler to bring the subject of conversation round to the Me 262, recommending its inclusion in the Reich air defences.

A typical conversation is recorded by Galland in his book:

> There was no beating about the bush with his answer when Hitler asked the commodore of JG Richthofen, Oberstleutnant Kurt Buhligen, if German fighters were inferior to those of the British and Americans: 'For two years we have been numerically inferior. Relatively speaking, our aircraft have now become slower. American and British fighters are about 70 kph faster than ours.' Hitler snapped back, 'What do you want then, a new aircraft?' At this, Johannes Steinhoff, whom Hitler had just decorated with the Swords to add to his Knight's Cross with Oak Leaves, butted in, 'Jawohl, the jet fighter!' Hitler gave a start and retorted brusquely, 'Fighter jet, fighter jet, it's a spook going round your heads. I won't hear any more of it! That is not a fighter and you will not be able to fight with it. My doctor has told me that in the sharp turns you have to make in dogfights, parts of the brain will simply separate. This aircraft is not yet mature and the fighter arm will not get it until it is. For you, I have instead healthier aircraft which have been developed on the basis of established technical experience.' Steinhoff, who would suffer severe burns a few months later during a failed Me 262 take-off, tried once more but was silenced with a single sentence. The consequence of this exchange was an order issued by both Hitler and Goering which strictly forbade any further mention of the words 'Me 262' and 'fighter' in the same breath.

With this, Galland had to accept that he could expect no further sympathy from Hitler for his concerns about the direction the air-war was taking. But he was still not yet prepared to yield. Given the situation on the various fronts and faced with an invasion of Europe which was probably imminent, he saw only one way to stop the rot or at least diminish it: fighters, fighters and more fighters. In this he knew that his staff stood with him shoulder to shoulder.

First he succeeded in obtaining the support of Armaments Minister Speer who agreed to divert to the fighter arm on a regular basis, and without Hitler's knowledge, a proportion of the Me 262 bomber output.

Galland's attempt to convince Reichsführer-SS Himmler of the decisive superiority of the Me 262 also bore fruit. Himmler, by now one of the most powerful men in the Third Reich, had for some time been aware that Goering was unable to provide the Luftwaffe with leadership in these critical months. That Goering's influence on Hitler had sunk to a minimum he knew already. The Waffen-SS was responsible for the V-weapons programme and large areas of aircraft production in bomb-proof underground installations and Himmler was keen to extend his influence into operational control of the Luftwaffe. Co-opting Himmler's aid was not received gladly in Luftwaffe circles, but for German fighter command affairs had deteriorated to the sorry pass where even Himmler was a welcome bedfellow in the campaign to exert pressure on Hitler to operate the Me 262 as a fighter.

When Goering saw Himmler's shadow beginning to eclipse him, he also began to speak out for a strengthening of Reich air defences by including the Me 262 within fighter ranks.

In the Messerschmitt factories and SS-run bomb-proof assembly plants there now began the hectic programme to follow the new plans for turning out the Me 262 fighter as a fast bomber. To extend its range two supplementary fuel tanks of 250 litres each were fitted beneath the pilot's seat. In the fuselage a 600-litre tank went behind what had been previously the main tank. This additional tank was the counterweight for the two 250-kg bombs slung below forward of the fuselage. Under normal circumstances aircrew would probably refuse to fly an aircraft cobbled together in this manner, even if the air force found it an acceptable addition to the fleet. Even without the possibility of encountering enemy aircraft it was problematic to fly the Me 262 bomber. Meticulous attention had to be paid to how the aircraft was manipulated. The particular problem was the rear 600-litre fuel tank. If this tank was full the aircraft was dangerously unstable without the bombs because the centre of gravity was too far back. Before dropping the bombs, however, the pilot had to ensure that the tank was empty. If he forgot this in the excitement of the moment or was forced to jettison the bombs in an emergency, the Me 262 became very tail-heavy and assumed an attitude out of the horizontal in which control could be lost. In turn the speed would drop to 700 kph or less, at which the aircraft was easy prey for a fighter. It was weakly armed in any case because two of the four machine-guns in the nose had been removed for weight reasons. Finally the Me 262 bomber had no bombsight and the pilot had to use the reflecting gunsight (*Reflexvisier* or REVI) for bomb-aiming in horizontal flight or a shallow dive. The instrument would have been useful in a steep dive but this form of attack was too dangerous to attempt. These circumstances were certain to lead to disaster – and they did.

The ten months of despair at the gates of hell between July 1944 and April 1945 were those least blessed by fortune and the most sacrificial in terms of casualties in the twelve years of existence of KG51 (formerly KG255, known as 'Edelweiss'). Nevertheless the exemplary fighting spirit of the entire squadron never faltered. I think it right to say that one should never identify, in any war, those who were 'the bravest', for the term cannot be applied to some without doing injustice to others. Bravery is a conquest of the fear with which we are all born. For some, great bravery is required just to be near the fighting front. The bravery of KG51 is chronicled in sixteen pages of the unit's War Diary.

When the squadron received orders to fly the Me 262 as a fast bomber, neither the commanders nor the pilots had had any preparatory training. Their joy over the undisputed advantages of the much praised new turbojet warbird was soon overshadowed by the suspicion which accompanies every unexpected boon. From the beginning of the war, bomber units had been in desperate need of an aircraft with adequate speed, a strong defensive armament and above all long range. Despite all the conversion work and modifications, the Me 262 was neither a Stuka nor a recognisable bomber aircraft. At low level it was so greedy on fuel that only targets over a short range fell within its ambit, and its speed, reduced by the bombload, no longer provided any significant advantage.

On 6 June 1944 the Allies landed on the coast of Normandy. Contrary to Hitler's plan and Goering's interpretation of how it would be on the night, the total number of bombs dropped by Me 262s was nil. The loading operations on the English side had proceeded unmolested, and there were no jet bombers 'smashing up all these heaps of material on the beaches' on the French side either. The reason was that all 3rd Squadron/KG51 pilots were undergoing conversion training to the Me 262 bomber at Lechfeld, following the completion of which they would deploy to the invasion front. The unit was known as Erprobungskommando Schenk after its commander, Major Wolfgang Schenk, holder of the Knight's Cross with Oak Leaves.

The KG51 *Edelweiss* War Diary records:

Quite a number of problems arose during the fitting out of the aircraft for bomber operations. At Schwäbisch Hall the undercarriage and tyres were strengthened and supplementary fuel tanks added. If care was not exercised in filling this tank it led to a hopeless shift in the centre of gravity leading to tail-heaviness and instability. There was no properly tested bomb retaining and release gear nor bombsights. In a shallow dive accuracy was poor. By order of the Führer, it was forbidden to dive-bomb, exceed 850 kph or descend below 12,000 feet over enemy-held territory. The last restriction was to provide enemy anti-aircraft batteries with less opportunity for a hit and thus to prevent any jet aircraft falling into enemy hands. It meant, however, that the project was doomed to fail from the start, and the poor bombing results were unavoidable and depressing. The infantry called us the 'Damage-the-Fields Squadron'. It was humorous but did not do much to raise our spirits. The restrictions were finally lifted in December 1944. Many Me 262 aircraft flown to Schwäbisch Hall for conversion fell victim to Allied air raids. At every step the *Sturmvögel* [storm petrel, a descriptive term for the Me 262 bomber] was hunted down. Every take-off, flight and landing was a minor suicide mission and gnawed away at the nerves …

While Erprobungskommando Schenk was re-training at Lechfeld, sixty Me 262 bombers were destroyed on the ground in an air raid, which introduced a lengthy delay to full operations. Not until 20 July 1944, six-and-a-half weeks after the invasion, did these twelve pilots of 3rd Squadron/KG51 complete the conversion course. Each had flown the aircraft four times, these being solo flights because it was a single-seater. The curriculum did not allow for bombing practice or even an introduction to fighter tactics. In this deplorable state of preparedness the unit was ordered with nine machines to Chateaudun from where it would fly operational missions against the English coast immediately upon arrival. The base was close to the French coast because the fast bomber only had a radius of action of 200 km, there being no latitude in fuel for the aircraft to fly out from a more rearward airfield. And it was at Chateaudun that the unique and miserable odyssey of 3rd Squadron/KG51 began – a unit obliged to pay in full for the Führer's obstinacy.

After six weeks of bombing the English coast, the squadron was forced back from Chateaudun to Etampes: from there three days later to Creil, where it stayed six days. This withdrawal seems to have been particularly hectic. Ground personnel were on the road day and night, constantly harassed by enemy fighter bombers. According to the KG51 War Diary, a lorry transporting several Me 262 jet turbines and spare parts was captured by an Allied unit. Thus it would appear that German turbojet engines were in American hands by August 1944. This was a serious loss to the unit, for engines had to be exchanged after eight hours' flying time for overhaul.

On the seventh day the Squadron arrived at Juvincourt where, on account of its losses, Schenk was obliged to request another nine pilots and aircraft. Of these, only five arrived at Juvincourt. Two crashed on take-off at Lechfeld because of pilot error, a third crashed landed at Schwäbisch Hall and the fourth set down in a meadow just short of the destination.

On 28 August 1944, Schenk's gradual homeward journey took another step eastwards to Ath-Chièvre in Belgium, from there on the 30th of the month the unit reached Volkel and Eindhoven in Holland for a five-day stay and after a flight in overnight fog put down on a Reich airfield at Rheine, Westphalia, on 3 September.

Erprobungskommando Schenk was here upgraded to I/KG51. As a squadron its operational aircraft had only been identified by a single capital letter on the fuselage but now also bore the tactical marking 9K before the black fuselage cross. Schenk was promoted to Oberstleutnant and took over command of the squadron, Major Grundmann led II/KG51 at Schwäbisch Hall. To consolidate the jet-bomber force the unit transferred next to Achmer and Hesepe where sections of KG76 flew operations against Allied targets in Belgium and Holland with the first twin-turbojet bomber, the Ar 234.

On 13 November 1944 the Allies mounted air raids on the bases at Rheine and Hesepe which took their toll of pilots and the almost irreplaceable engineers and technical support staff. Little mention is ever made of the part played by the men and women in these and other unglamorous roles such as radar direction. Such servicemen, for whom no better name has been found than 'ground personnel', served with a devotion to duty no less laudable than that of the pilots.

Many Me 262 fliers were cruelly cut down in a fiasco following the early morning attack known as Operation Bodenplatte on New Year's Day 1945. At 03:00 800 German aircraft took off to bomb Allied airfields, bases, anti-aircraft emplacements and bridgeheads in France, Belgium and Holland. 810 enemy aircraft were destroyed together with workshops, fuel dumps and valuable materials. It made no difference to the outcome of the battle, and 293 German machines shot down was a high price to pay for a surprise raid which the enemy side had not expected. The attack had been carefully prepared and kept secret until immediately before take-off. The plan was so secret that it omitted instructions to inform the German flak batteries of what was afoot and these gunned down no fewer than 200 German aircraft returning from the mission. 'Points glowing red in the snow marked where they crashed,' was the laconic observation of the KG51 War Diary.

After US forces captured the bridge at Remagen on 7 March 1945, Goering telephoned the I/KG51 orderly officer that night ordering him personally to comb through the unit without delay in search for 'volunteers who, following the example of Japanese kamikaze pilots, would dive their aircraft into the Rhine bridges so as to deny these valuable bridgeheads to the Americans.' Two pilots actually did volunteer but fortunately for them nothing came of this pointless notion, nor of the suggestion to Me 163 squadron JG400 made at about the same time when volunteers were invited to come forward as ramming pilots. This order also came from Goering.[4]

In the last eight weeks of the war, the senselessness of using a fighter aircraft like the Me 262 as a bomber proved itself to the full. The only positive thing to come of it all was that the devotion to duty and the fighting spirit of pilots and ground personnel alike continued to the last day. The epitaph to the Me 262 as a bomber aircraft appears in a single sentence of the KG51 War Diary:

> During the relatively short operational period flying the Me 262, 172 Squadron members were killed: 53 officers, 91 NCOs and 28 men.

The early reported shortcomings of the Me 262 as a fast bomber reinforced the concerns over its obvious unsuitability as a conversion for the role, but there was still a long way to go before Hitler finally recognised it. The useless early sacrifices confirmed the opinion long held in the offices of General der Jagdflieger Galland, and his more recent converts Speer and Himmler. Meanwhile enemy bomber streams flowed in and out of the Reich day and night. In a single attack on Lechfeld alone, sixty operational Me 262s were destroyed on the ground.

Kommando 262 Thierfelder, now reduced to a very small team of six operational pilots, could claim twenty-five enemy aircraft shot down, a noteworthy achievement. Günther Wegmann was Thierfelder's adjutant. While Wörner saw to the conversion training of newly arrived men, Thierfelder, Wegmann and four other pilots made the operational test flights. The prime target was enemy reconnaissance machines and successes proved the Me 262 to be an excellent fighter aircraft once its peculiarities had been mastered. Within the framework of the Reich air-defence system as a whole, the successes of these first Me 262 fighter pilots were not significant. It was only when the statisticians measured the victories per aircraft and expressed the figure proportionally that it was at once evident why the aircraft merited the trust of fighter pilots and their command staffs. And more than that, it suggested how much greater the overall successes would have been had Hitler and Goering given the machine the highest priority from its debut.

In July 1944 Galland managed to obtain authority to operate a second small Kommando 262 over central Germany. That this was possible was due in no small measure to the successes of Thierfelder's unit and not least to Alfred Schreiber. Wegmann was appointed to lead it and once Kommando Wegmann was in existence, it was to transfer to Erfurt-Bindersleben.

On 18 July, a fine summer's day, Thierfelder took off for a test flight. Onlookers watched his aircraft gather ever more speed along the runway, lift off about two-thirds of the way along and, after a few seconds of level flight, soar into the almost cloudless sky at a steep rate of climb. The Me 262 was then not visible until condensation trails began to form behind it. After a while it was observed that the aircraft was put into a shallow dive which gradually became ever steeper. At this point a witness stated that he thought he saw flames. The jet was in a virtual nose-dive when an object came free – possibly the cabin hood – and quickly afterwards a dark bundle emerged. Within three seconds the silk of a parachute began to inflate and then both the aircraft and pilot were lost to sight.

They found Hauptmann Thierfelder in a field near Buchloe. He was dead in the harness of his parachute. The canopy was in long ribbons, the material apparently having failed to withstand the opening stresses at deployment. The team puzzled over the possible cause of this accident for many days, for Thierfelder knew the Me 262 in all its moods and had proved himself an exceptionally apt pilot for the machine. The best explanation seemed to be fire in one or both turbojets which Thierfelder had perhaps tried to extinguish by diving the aircraft at high speed. It might then have wandered into an almost vertical dive from which there was no hope of recovery. On the other hand, possibly the trim was wrong. There were many possibilities. Thierfelder's successor as commander was Hauptmann Horst Geyer.

Wegmann's new unit was of squadron size, about ten aircraft. At Bindersleben they had their hands full with adapting the aerodrome for the Me 262. Both runways had to be extended from 1,200 to 1,500 yards, mechanics' equipment rigged up in the hangars and a radar direction centre built on the northern fringe of the airfield. The work lasted into September 1944 when the Kommando was suddenly ordered to Achmer, the airfield at Rheine north of Osnabruck from where Kommando Schenk's Me 262 bombers operated. Wegmann's annoyance can be imagined, for he and his men had spent a great deal of time and energy expanding and fitting out Bindersleben.

The purpose of the move was to merge the two units at Lechfeld and Bindersleben into a single larger Kommando of which Major Nowotny was to be the unit leader. Whereas Goering had ordered the transfer, the order certainly did not originate from him, for he did not have the authority to arrange a change of this nature at the time without Hitler's express approval. Accordingly it seems probable that Hitler had caved in slightly to Galland's persistence. The Führer had not actually changed his mind: the events of recent months had forced him to bend a little. These events can be summarised as follows.

On 20 and 21 May 1944 the Allies destroyed the German synthetic fuel plants and attacked Berlin with an air fleet consisting of 1,500 bombers and 1,000 fighters. On 22 May the Soviet Army began its summer offensive under an umbrella of 4,000 aircraft.

After the violent verbal exchange between Hitler and Generalfeldmarschall Milch at the Berghof on 24 May 1944, the future of the Me 262 as a lame-duck bomber seemed certain. On the 29th, Oberst Gollob, Galland's staff officer with responsibility for the Me 262 fighter, was relieved of the portfolio by Goering who transferred it to General der Kampfflieger, Generalleutnant Peltz. At about the same time, Oberst Petersen advised Milch that the whole field of aircraft production, which was until then Milch's responsibility, was being transferred to the newly appointed Chief of the Fighter Staff, Karl-Otto Saur, Speer's deputy. That signalled the end of Milch's role as Goering's Plenipotentiary which he had held since the summer of 1941.

On 7 June 1944, the day following the Normandy landings, Hitler ordered an increase in Me 262 and Do 335 production. During the Invasion, aircraft of the Allied air forces flew 14,700 missions compared with 319 of the Luftwaffe. On 19 June, Milch found out that he was to be relieved of his office. His request to resign as Secretary of State and Minister for Aircraft Production was approved by Hitler with the result that the office devolved upon Speer and Saur. On 25 June Hitler demanded a greater effort in the fight to reduce Allied air superiority and asked Saur how many fighters could be turned out each month if production work on the He 177 bomber were suspended. Saur told him about a thousand. On 27 June Goering ordered a halt to bomber production. When General Köller protested, Goering told him, 'It is the will of the Führer that only fighters are to be built from now on.' On two occasions, immediately after the attempt on Hitler's life on 20 July 1944 and again on 30 August, General Kreipe solicited Hitler's agreement for the exclusive deployment of the Me 262 as a fighter. Hitler made a brusque refusal each time. At the end of August Hitler circulated throughout the Luftwaffe a Führer-edict which every officer was obliged to sign. This order read: 'With immediate effect I forbid anybody to speak to me about the Me 262 jet aircraft in any other connection or any other role than as a fast or Blitzbomber.'

Nine months for possible Me 262 fighter operations had been lost up to the time when Kommando Nowotny was formed. Without question these nine months were decisive for the seizure of air supremacy over the Reich by the Allies, the precondition for the total defeat of Hitler's Germany. Hitler may have sensed that for himself when he suddenly began to demand 'Fighters! Fighters! Only fighters!'[5]

Hitler's resistance crumbled further in mid-September 1944. Major Walther Dahl had set up IV *Sturmgruppe* within JG3 Udet in May 1944. Once operational in September, after only two days this piston-engined fighter group initially produced astounding successes pitted as they were against a numerically superior enemy force of bombers and fighters. This led to corresponding Allied countermeasures such that the unit was hard hit by a sudden reversal of fortune on the third day. In his remarkable book *Rammjäger* Dahl described it thus: with Dahl leading his Sturmgruppe on 11 September 1944, they shot down 170 enemy aircraft (95 bombers, 75 fighters) for only 3 German losses. On 12 September the tally was 100 enemy aircraft (87 bombers, 13 fighters) for 13 German losses. On 13 September the Allied bomber formation lost 24 aircraft (7 bombers, 17 fighters) for the loss of 36 German aircraft. The reversal was caused by the Allied air force having strengthened the fighter escort substantially. On account of this adverse swing in the fortunes of his unit, Major Dahl was summoned at once over Goering's head to Hitler's HQ. In his book he records:

I arrived at Führer HQ Wolfschanze in East Prussia and was taken to the so-called situations room where I waited for Hitler… suddenly I saw a figure entering the bunker with a tired walk, bent as if carrying a heavy burden. It was Hitler!

The Luftwaffe ADC, Oberst von Below, introduced me and I reported myself. Hitler offered me his hand and said warmly, 'I am pleased to see you here. I have already heard much about you and the efforts of the brave men of your squadron. Your *Sturmgruppen* (fighter assault groups) have made a decisive contribution and I am proud to have such pilots in the Luftwaffe.' With a gesture he invited me to take an armchair. I sat directly opposite him. He came at once to our three engagements of 11 to 13 September, the actual reason for my presence. I had to describe exactly the course of each air-battle and especially that of 'the black 13 September'. During the session of question and answer with Hitler, the no. 1 problem of the Luftwaffe, the Me 262, was constantly at the back of my mind. Somehow I had to bring the topic of conversation round to this theme despite the Führer-edict of the month before.

As Hitler began speaking about our heavy losses of 13 September, he attributed them to the numerical superiority of the bombers. I saw my chance. 'The enemy fighters are our greatest danger in the air,' I said, 'and only fast, very fast, aircraft can win us the opportunity to strip away from formations the enemy fighter cover so that the bombers can be attacked unmolested.' Tensely I waited for his reaction. He gave me a searching look and then his gruff voice replied, 'You mean the Me 262. Say what you want to.' I knew that my opinion contradicted his own but I attempted to convince Hitler by argument. During the resulting discussion, Hitler astonished me with his precise knowledge of technical details. At the end of our talk, which lasted almost three hours, I had the feeling that my opinion was not without its echo. Some time later the order came down that a proportion of Me 262 was to be re-scheduled for the fighter arm.

Galland was overjoyed. To some extent he now had a free hand and nominated as commander of the combined Kommando 262 Thierfelder–Wegmann the best available man, Austrian-born Major Walter Nowotny, with 256 kills to his credit the second most successful fighter pilot after Erich Hartmann. Besides being a proven and thoroughly capable wing leader, he knew how to nurse inexperienced young pilots through their first combat missions. In view of the sizeable contingent of pilots in Kommando Nowotny fresh from training school, that seemed to Galland a point of no small importance.

In his letter to me dated 26 January 1977 responding to my request for information, Adolf Galland recounted the inside story of many events related in this book, principally the setting-up of the Kommando Nowotny, and its last day of operations. I re-produce here the pertinent abstract from the letter because it shows how the formation of Kommando Nowotny coincides closely with the political manoeuvring referred to earlier in this chapter. In September 1944 Galland had received from Goering the order:

…to set up forthwith an operational Kommando from the two manufacturer's test units, and locate it on the Western Front. Apparently this was done on Himmler's advice that it was a simple way of providing evidence in the form of aerial combat victories that the Me 262 was an outstanding fighter aircraft. My objection that the development was too rapid and that this unit would be better defending the Reich from within was unsuccessful. I appointed Major Nowotny commander of the unit and told him to operate from Achmer near Rheine. Here, under the the most difficult circumstances, aided by a constant fighter umbrella to protect the runways at Achmer and Hesepe, he achieved good results but also sustained losses. I mention particularly a large number of losses attributable to technical faults and errors for which the ground personnel were partially responsible. On the day when he destroyed a Mustang and was himself shot down after a turbine failure, I was an onlooker. By telephone I ordered the withdrawal to Brandenburg-Briest and sent the pilots to Lechfeld for further training. It was from this unit, however, that the best jet Group, III/JG7, came into being...'

Professor Willy Messerschmitt (1898–1978), designer of the Me 262.

Flugkapitän Fritz Wendel, chief test pilot, Messerschmitt AG Augsburg.

Above: A montage depicting two Me 262A-1a fighters. The nearer aircraft, works number 110522, was flown by Fritz Wendel at Lechfeld as part of III/EJG2 and later with Nowotny's Kommando.

Below: An Me 262 in England after the war.

The cockpit of the Me 262:
(1) Instrument panel (2) Blind flying equipment (Ed: NB-perhaps he means panel far left. Tr.) (3) Speedometer (4) Artificial horizon (5) Variometer (6) Altimeter (7) Main daughter compass (8) AFN2 (9) SZKK2 (10) Revolutions indicator (11) Gas pressure gauge (12) Gas temperature indicators (13) Pressure gauge (injection) (14) Pressure gauge (lubricant) (15) Fuel gauge (forward tanks) (16) Fuel gauge (rear tanks) (17) ZSK 244A (only fitted to aircraft on Blitzbomber operations).

Test pilot Erich Warsitz made the first flight with the Heinkel rocket aircraft He 176 on 20 June 1939. On 27 August 1939 he piloted the first jet-turbine prototype, the He 178, on its maiden flight. Two German successes on the grandiose scale destined never to be used.

Above: The He 178. *Below:* An artist's impression of the He 178 in flight.

Hauptmann Walter Nowotny.

With sixteen victories,
Oberstleutnant Heinz Bär,
commander EJG2, was one of
the two most successful jet-
fighter pilots of the Second
World War.

On the runway at Lechfeld, Hauptmann Wolfgang Späte, who test-flew the prototypes for the Reich Air Ministry, speaks to Adolf Galland and Willy Messerschmitt.

General der Jagdflieger Adolf Galland on 22 May 1943 discussing with test pilot Fritz Wendel the qualities of the Me 262 after having flown the aircraft for the first time: 'It feels as though there's an angel pushing it.'

Above: Udet (far left) with Goering, Willy Messerschmitt and Rakan Kokothaki evidently in high spirits during an exhibition of the Me 262.

Centre: In the presence of Willy Messerschmitt, Goering takes his leave in front of the Messerschmitt AG administration building after a visit.

Below: Pilot Gerd Lindner reporting his immediate findings to Goering after an Me 262 test flight.

Top left: Oberleutnant Günther Wegmann at Schwabstadl near Lechfeld in July 1944.

Top right: Oberst Edgar Petersen, head of the Luftwaffe Test Centre, Rechlin, in conversation with Adolf Galland.

Left: Major Rudolf Sinner, left hand and face heavily bandaged after being shot down on 4 April 1945, is escorted by Hauptmann Streiber to the aircraft which took him to Salzburg Military Hospital.

Below: Jochen Marseille discussing the Me 262 with test pilot Fritz Wendel while Me 163 pilot, Austrian Joschi Pohs looks on.

Willy Messerschmitt explaining a point about the Me 262 to Adolf Hitler and Ernst Udet.

Oberst Gordon Gollob, successor to Galland as General der Jagdflieger.

Top: Me 262A-1a fighter, works number 170059, delivered to Thierfelder's EKdo 262 at Lechfeld on 20 August 1944 and allocated to Leutnant Fritz Müller. The aircraft was later transferred to I/KG(J)54.

Centre: Graveyard of German aircraft: in the foreground two wrecked Me 262s, behind is a Ju 88 and other aircraft.

Below: Oberfeldwebel Rumler (with peaked cap standing on wing) at Perleberg on 15 April 1945 during an intermediate stop.

Oberleutnant Kurt Welter, Staffelkapitän 10/NJG 11, was the 769th recipient of the Oak Leaves to the Knight's Cross. His *Welterkommando Me 262* obtained its success in the searchlight beams of Berlin. Welter was probably the top-scoring jet-fighter ace with twenty victories.

'FE' means Foreign Evaluation. This Me 262B-1a, two-seater night fighter equipped with an SN-2 Lichtenstein radar, was captured undamaged by the Americans. Possibly Kurt Welter flew it once or twice.

Above: An Me 262 night fighter being serviced prior to operations.

Below: Four Messerschmitt test pilots: Theo Tumborn, Fritz Wendel, Hermann Wurster, Sepp Sinz.

Above: Twelve R4M rockets carried in a rack below each wing and fired in salvoes achieved a good scatter and proved the most accurate and effective armament of the jet fighter. An aircraft so fitted was re-designated Me 262A-1aR1 or R7.

Below: The only Me 262 to be armed with a modified Rheinmetall BK5 50 mm anti-tank cannon. Here the ammunition belt is being loaded with 5-cm shells. The gun was to be used in the anti-bomber role but was never used operationally.

Above: The Inspector of Day-fighters, Oberstleutnant Hannes Trautloft, with Erich Hohagen, who has just landed after a training flight. Between the two commodores of EJG2 (Ergänzungs-jadggeschwader 2) is Oberstleutnant Werner Andres. Extreme left is Hauptmann Georg Eder, at the right with his back to the camera Oberleutnant Wörner.

Below: Erich Hohagen in the cockpit before taking off. He wore a protective cap following his serious head injury. Assisting him buckle up is his personal ground crewman.

Above left: Staffelkapitän Oberleutnant Franz Schall, Kommando Nowotny and III/JG7, issuing his instructions by field telephone.

Above right: Cameraman Karl W Lüttgau, Messerschmitt Works photographer, made the Me 262 training films.

Below: Ground crew and pilots of Erprobungskommando Me 262 turn out for a soccer match. On the right are the future pilots of the Kommando Nowotny and III/JG7.

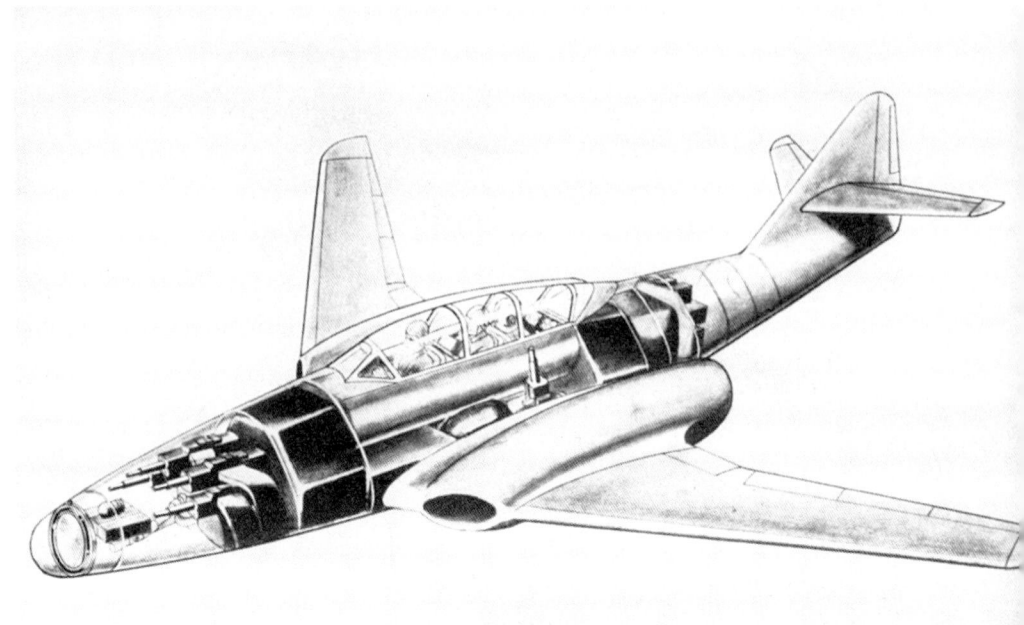

Above: War's end design for a three-seater Messerschmitt night-fighter equipped with two Heinkel S-011 jet turbines.

Below: Shortly before the capitulation, Messerschmitt test pilots Gerd Lindner, Karl Baur (chief pilot) and Ludwig Hofmann share a joke with a Luftwaffe officer during a pause from flying at Lechfeld.

8

Clashes over the Western Front
Late 1944

At the end of 1943, Allied air intelligence was well informed regarding the development and readiness of the Me 163 rocket fighter. Aerodromes identified as their operational stations were regularly overflown and photographed by reconnaissance aircraft from the beginning of 1944 and so it came as no surprise to Allied air force commands when these strange machines made their debut in the skies over Germany. On the other hand, pilots and aircrew of USAAF and RAF aircraft had not been forewarned of the existence of the Me 163. The report by Rust and Hess regarding the first encounter between a Spitfire and Me 163 at the end of June 1944 relates:

> At an altitude of about 30,000 feet the Spitfire pilot –
> climbing to 37,000 – saw about 7,000 feet behind him a con-
> densation trail rising very fast from below. It was a day of
> perfect visibility without cloud so that the British pilot
> assumed he was about to be engaged by a Luftwaffe fighter.
> He continued his climb, and at about 41,000 feet saw the
> other aircraft only 3,000 feet behind and at the same altitude.
> He noticed how the condensation trail of the enemy machine
> disappeared and then reappeared several times [a typical
> characteristic of the Me 163 when the spirit level for the
> rocket motor was almost drained]. His attempt to identify the
> enemy was unsuccessful. It seemed to him to be a flying wing
> type never previously seen. The German machine was 3,000

feet below him but only 1,000 feet astern and meant that it had gained 8,000 feet in height in the period that the Spitfire had climbed 4,000 feet full out. Seconds later he lost sight of the German aircraft since no condensation trail was visible. [This is proof that it was an Me 163, probably from Brandis near Leipzig. The rocket motor ran for only five to six minutes before the fuel was burnt up and then the condensation trail also petered out.]

In July 1944 the first encounter occurred between a British aircraft and an Me 262 over Munich, as reported by the crew of a De Havilland Mosquito, was equally dangerous but finished bloodless:

During a reconnaissance flight at 29,000 feet pilot Lt Wall and observer Flying Officer Lobham sighted a fast-approaching twin-engined machine barely 400 yards behind them. This was disconcerting, because never previously had they known of an enemy aircraft able to outpace a Mosquito. Upon receiving his observer's warning, Wall put the throttle to full. The strange aircraft came rapidly closer, however, rose up a little and then took station behind the Mosquito a little off centre to starboard. As the Me 262 – now recognised as such – attempted to straighten up to shoot, Wall saved his own machine by banking sharply right. He could not shake off his opponent, however, which within a minute was again behind him and after narrowing the gap opened fire at 700 yards. Wall made a slight turn to avoid the danger and then banked as tightly as he could, a manoeuvre which got him behind the German jet. At once the Me 262 shed height to disengage.

The jousting was repeated three times over without the German pilot managing to obtain a hit. On the fifth close pass, with the Me 262 extremely near, the Mosquito escaped once more by a very acute turn. Wall heard two dull thumps in the fuselage and, assuming they had been hit, ordered Lobham to open the emergency hatch in readiness to bale out. While manipulating the inside handle, Lobham noticed that the hatch cover had torn free at the hinges and disappeared. This accounted for the dull thuds Wall had heard. The pilot had had enough. He put his aircraft into a steep dive and sought the protection of cumulus at 16,000 feet. When the Mosquito emerged three or four minutes later, there was no sign of the Me 262, and the British machine returned safely to its operational base at Fermo near Venice.

The interesting report by Rust and Hess, though concerned mainly with US 8th Air Force operations over Reich territory for the month from 7 October 1944, coincides in many aspects with the narrative in the last chapter and an abridged version is repeated here.

On 7 October over Holland and Germany 8th Air Force exchanged fire on about 25 occasions with German jets. These were all Me 262s with the exception of four Me 163 rocket fighters which attacked B-17s over Leipzig. There were several victories to report. Mustang pilot Lieutenant Urban L Drew became the first US pilot to shoot down two jets on the same day. These were the Me 262s of Leutnant Gerhard Kobert (works number 110405) and Oberleutnant Paul Bley (works number 170307). The two German aircraft had just taken off when Drew surprised them at 1,000 feet and shot both down. Bley baled out safely but his wingman was killed. The other pair of the four got away and climbed to intercept the American formation. A third machine destroyed by Colonel Hubert Zemke and Lieutenant Norman Benolt was taken to be an Me 109. Only later, when the film recording the incident was examined, was the German aircraft identified correctly as an Me 262. During a dive at about 800 kph the American fighters' fire sheared off the port wing of the Me 262 of Oberfahnrich Heinz Russel (works number 110395). The ensign though wounded landed safely by parachute.

On 13 October an Me 262 Blitzbomber from Kommando Schenk, of Unteroffizier Edmund Delatowski (works number 170064), was shot down by a Hawker Tempest of 3 Squadron RAF over Holland. The British aircraft was at 15,000 feet over Volkel when the pilot noticed a condensation trail approaching. He identified it as a fast-closing Me 262 whose pilot opened fire and missed with two longish bursts when slightly above the British fighter. The German machine passed within 40 yards of the Tempest which gave chase concealed within the condensation cloud. When the jet made a 180-degree turn in a shallow dive, the Tempest followed suit. In the attempt to shake off the British aircraft the Blitzbomber gained about 900 feet in altitude before pulling out in a right-hand turn. This enabled the British pilot to close in at 10,000 feet, reduce speed a little to line up the target and fire. The first burst at 300 yards missed, but after closing to 80 yards he poured a full burst into the German jet which 'exploded like a flying bomb' and disintegrated. If this Blitzbomber was actually carrying a large bomb, the narrative serves to illustrate how poorly the aircraft handled with a payload. The remains of the 262 spun to the ground although its Unteroffizier appears to have been thrown clear, for he survived. Over the next four months the Tempests of 122 Wing RAF shot down six Me 262s and an Ar 234.

For the US 8th Air Force, November 1944 was a month of many encounters with German jets: their fighters reported 137 contacts with a duel resulting on 29 occasions. They shot down 11 jets and damaged seven others in the air. 41 were destroyed and 17 damaged on the ground. 8th Air Force bombers had 53 encounters, fire being exchanged on 13 occasions. One Me 262 was shot down plus one probable and one destroyed on the ground. Known US losses to German jets were two fighters and no bombers.

On 1 November weather conditions were unfavourable for large-scale bomber operations and only 318 heavy bombers took off. Their targets were two synthetic oil factories at Gelsenkirchen and the Hindenburg bridge over the Rhine at Rudesheim. B-17 bombers of the 11th Division reached Gelsenkirchen unopposed but were challenged over Holland on the homeward flight by Me 262 (works number 110386) piloted by Oberfahnrich Willi Banzhaff who had sighted the bomber formation with its fighter escort from about 36,000 feet.

Descending to 30,000 feet, at 14:12 hours Banzhaff attacked the leading group of fighters from the rear. In a perfectly executed 30-degree dive he reached Yellow Flight and fired on Lieutenant Debbis J Allison's Mustang which almost at once fell away in flames. Banzhaff, with 20th Fighter Group Mustangs in hot pursuit, now continued his dive intending to engage the Fortress formation.

The opening phase of the struggle had been observed by 56th Fighter Group pilots flying Thunderbolts as escort to a Liberator bomber formation. Together with a flight of Mustangs from 352nd Fighter Group they detached at once to join in the pursuit of the lone German aircraft. It seemed as if this overwhelming force would soon be squabbling within its own ranks for the privilege of ridding the skies of Banzhaff.

The German pilot was aware of the size of the opposing crowd on his tail. He pulled out of his dive at 9,000 feet, made a 180-degree turn at full throttle and headed northwards for a layer of cloud he had spotted over the Zuider Zee. He reached it and escaped for a while the three groups of fighters. His error was the turn, for the Thunderbolts and some of the Mustangs had cut him off and were now lurking around the bank of cloud, awaiting his reappearance. As he emerged he was greeted by a hail of fire from every American aircraft cannon which could be brought to bear. The Me 262 sustained numerous hits to its port wing and fuselage but without apparent ill effect.

Banzhaff had no alternative but to take them all on. All the American fighters had far longer endurance than he and at some time within the hour he would have to attempt a landing. Lieutenant Flowers of the 20th Fighter Group was hit by the German's fire while executing a tight turn, Lieutenant Gerbe and three other American fighters all suffered damage at the ensign's hands. 56 Group/63 Squadron pilot Lieutenant Groce shouted over his radio, 'Break off! We'll get him when he makes his next turn!' Shortly after, the harried Banzhaff made a left turn while climbing which brought him momentarily overhead of Lieutenant Groce's fighter. The latter took advantage of the favourable shooting position and hit Banzhaff's starboard turbine, which exploded. The Me 262 began immediately to spin downwards out of control and Willi Banzhaff baled out a few moments later. The jet crashed between Enschede and Zwolle in Holland. All six American pilots in the vicinity claimed the highly prized kill of an Me 262, but it was awarded at debriefing half each to Groce and Gerbe of 352nd

Fighter Group. Banzhaff landed safely by parachute.

On 2 November two Me 262s attacked the 2nd B-24 Bomber Wing over Bielefeld at between 21,000 to 24,000 feet. This was the first known attack using the R4M rocket battery. A Thunderbolt of 56th Group was shot down. This seemed a mere sideshow, for 400 German propeller fighters had made their appearance late that morning and a massive air-battle developed with the 8th Air Force bombers and fighter escort.

On 4 November 8th Air Force Thunderbolts and Mustangs flying bomber protection reported being attacked by various Me 262s operating in pairs which went for the fighter escort and ignored the bombers. The Americans claimed no victories on this day although the Luftwaffe admitted the loss of an Me 262 (works number 110483), shot down by an RAF fighter near Lüneburg. Thus perished the brave Oberfahnrich Willi Banzhaff.

On 6 November two German jets were shot down by Captain Charles E Yeager (the pilot accredited with being the first through the sound barrier in 1947) and Lieutenant William J Quinn. The latter was wingman to Captain Montgomery over Germany when two Me 262s were sighted 6,000 feet below. 'One of the two German aircraft banked towards me suddenly,' Quinn reported, 'and I opened fire immediately and hit his cockpit. Parts of the machine broke off before it fell and crashed into the ground.' This was the Me 262 (works number 110490) of Oberfeldwebel Helmut Lennartz, who got out safely. Captain Montgomery destroyed an Me 262 in a hangar, and Yeager two others on the ground. The aircraft shot down by Yeager (works number 110389) was Leutnant Spangenberg's; he survived.

8 November 1944 was the last day of operations for Kommando Nowotny. Four of its jets were shot down. The first casualty was Wegmann's wingman Oberfeldwebel Baudach, shot down flying works number 900036 by Anthony Maurice of 361st Fighter Group. Baudach lived to tell the tale. The second American victory was reported by 20th Fighter Group when Captain Ernest C Fiebelkorn and the Mustang pilot of another group attacked an Me 262 together as it was taking off. While the Americans were attempting to line up the target, the jet began to spin out of control

and exploded without a shot having been fired. This was Schall's wingman, Feldwebel Erich Büttner, flying works number 170293. Büttner baled out safely.

The third jet was lost in the following manner. Lieutenant James W Kenney, 357th Group/362nd Fighter Squadron, had been ordered to escort to their home airfield another Mustang whose pilot had become concerned at the roughness of his aircraft's engine. On the return flight over western Germany in dense cloud they caught up with a formation of 13 Fortresses, and as these bombers had no fighter escort the two Mustangs took on the role for as long as the suspect Mustang engine would hold out. Oberleutnant Schall had just broken off from an engagement against the bombers and overtook the two fighters without noticing them. The Americans got him in their sights and opened fire.

Schall's aircraft was hit in the port wing and engine but Schall interpreted this as a turbine malfunction. He was attempting to restart the engine when suddenly he spotted the two Mustangs on his tail. Flames began to issue from the damaged turbojet and Schall put the aircraft into a left-angled dive before parachuting free. His Me 262 with only one engine would have been easy pickings for the Mustangs. (Schall landed safely. He was killed on 10 April 1945 while attempting to land an Me 262 of JG7 on a bomb-damaged runway.)

The fourth Me 262 to be lost on 8 November 1944 was Nowotny's (works number 110400). None of the thirty pilots who chased him claimed to have destroyed the jet initially but it seems to have been awarded as a probable to Lieutenant R W Stevens, 364th Fighter Group. It is known that Nowotny attacked a bomber stream escorted by Mustangs and had several of the latter on his tail. In his final radio message reported in an earlier chapter, he claimed three kills, said he had lost his port engine and was under attack. His next sentence was garbled, but seconds later his aircraft began its death dive with a loud screaming noise, burst into flames and hit the ground about 6 kilometres north of Bramsche before Nowotny could get out. (This account was supplied by the American writer Patrick J Cassidy Jr and coincides with a report in Luftwaffe files submitted by Oberleutnant Hans Dortenmann, V/JG54.)

9

The Loss of Nowotny

The aircraft of the Bindersleben 262 Kommando touched down at Achmer almost at the same time as Nowotny's flight. Günther Wegmann handed over his unit and was appointed Nowotny's adjutant immediately. The new, larger Kommando was now reorganised into 8th Squadron at Hesepe under Leutnant Schall and 9th Squadron under Oberleutnant Bley at Achmer. A mountain of work awaited everybody. Nowotny confirmed his reputation as an energetic organiser. All day and every day he occupied his time telephoning or visiting the local Gauleiter, the offices of General Galland, the Reich Air Ministry, the Messerschmitt people and equipment suppliers with a view to getting the unit operational as early as possible. His major demands were for more ground personnel, more aircraft, more modern equipment, more pilots. There was not a moment's peace until the radar direction unit was set up in a small guesthouse between the two airfields and Viktor Preusker was installed there as master of ceremonies. It was recognised that it was likely that enemy intelligence knew about Nowotny's Kommando from the outset. Its location lay below the path of the main bomber approach routes to Berlin and other cities and the low-flying Mustangs which controlled the local air space soon made their presence felt. The German unit received a bitter foretaste of just how dangerous this spot would be on its first day of operations.

On the afternoon of 7 October 1944 warning was given of large bomber formations approaching. Four Me 262s were sent up to intercept. Two were shot down by Mustangs while climbing away from the runway. The third and fourth got among the bombers, destroying three, possibly four. On their return both jets were low on fuel. One landed safely, the other was shot by Mustangs while landing. Despite a great hail of flak and the presence of German conventional fighters guarding the airfield approaches three Me 262s had been lost. Taking off and landing, the jets were at their most vulnerable to the ever-watchful Mustangs; it was not the first time it had happened in the history of the Me 262 but for Nowotny it was a savage blow. The problem was primarily having the airfield in the path of the enemy bomber streams; the Mustang advance guard waited for the jets to rise and simply gobbled them up.

The next operation came two days later. The Kommando got off more lightly but the circumstances were disquieting. After a successful mission Leutnant Schall was pursued home by a swarm of Mustangs and shot down. He baled out and was then ruthlessly machine-gunned by the American fighters while dangling from his parachute. This was against the rules of warfare.[6]

Schall was extraordinarily lucky and landed unharmed. Upon receiving his report, Nowotny was beside himself with rage: his personal code was one of strict compliance with the rules of warfare and he had never understood the need to continue a dog-fight once the opposing pilot had been deprived of his machine. So overcome was he that when a Mustang pilot was brought in after parachuting from his aircraft two days later, Nowotny ordered his adjutant Wegmann to have the American taken out and shot. By now Wegmann understood Nowotny's passionate temperament and decided that the order was rhetorical. The same day the American was safely behind the barbed wire of a PoW camp. During a relaxed talk in the officers' mess on the evening of 5 November 1944 Nowotny thanked his adjutant for disobeying the order. Wegmann and Oberleutnant Schnörrer then discussed with the commander the disadvantages of having the joint airfields directly below the bomber path. Next the question was explored of improving the Me 262. Here the most urgent modifications were a lengthened control stick for more leverage to bring the aircraft out of a steep dive and better armament.

On account of his many belly-landings and parachute escapes twenty-five-year-old Karl Schnörrer was nicknamed 'Quax' after the Ruhmann cartoon character of the time 'Quax the Crash Landing Pilot'. He had flown 500 missions, about half as Nowotny's wingman, and the men were good friends. Quax and Wegmann had therefore both been 'baptised in the waters of all fronts' as the saying went. The stormy Nowotny set great store by Schnörrer's judgment. After the war, the latter admitted that he was personally not comfortable with the Me 262, knowing it not to have been thoroughly tested and lacking essential equipment early on.

Once the various technical subjects had been talked over to exhaustion, Nowotny's companions toasted his first Me 262 victory the previous day, the 257th kill of his career. After the glasses had been emptied, Nowotny's mood became morose. 'It's a funny thing,' he said at length, 'but I keep having this dream about my next victory. Suddenly there's one right behind me. You know the bomber I shot down yesterday? I had seen that happen in a dream beforehand too. Last night I didn't dream at all.' After a lengthy pause he added, more to himself than his two listeners, 'Perhaps the next will be the last.' It sounded so odd to hear Nowotny speak in this manner that both Wegmann and Schnörrer had to force a laugh.

'Now, now, Nowi, don't talk such utter rot,' Schnörrer chided him, 'You, of all people! If ever I spoke like that I'd have to have a pretty good reason for doing so, not a dream.' He took the decanter and filled the empty glasses. 'Now, let's drink to the next half dozen!'

Nowotny was expecting the visit of the Inspector of Day-fighters, Oberst Hannes Trautloft, next day. Trautloft's job was to monitor the standards of upkeep of the day-fighter units, of which the Me 262 now formed part. A successful fighter pilot since the beginning of the campaign in Spain in 1936, he had been one of the first Me 109 pilots and was thus an old hand who knew how to get things done better than anybody. He heard out Nowotny's concerns sympathetically and then summoned a conference to listen to the requests of the Kommando's pilots. Heading the list was the need for constant Fw 190 and Me 109 fighter protection above Hesepe and Achmer. Trautloft had been commodore of

Nowotny's training squadron and that evening they sat in pleasant reminiscences of better times. It was their last reunion.

During the early afternoon of the next day, 7 November 1944, General Galland and Generaloberst Alfred Keller arrived by air at short notice. Keller, a commander of very long experience, had had charge of IV Fliegerkorps over Holland and Belgium in May 1940. As General der Flieger he had attempted to dissuade Hitler from invading the Soviet Union. Afterwards he commanded Air Fleet 1 against Leningrad. At the time of his visit to Achmer he was responsible for producing the new generation of German military aviators and had had the opportunity to witness at first hand the Me 262 training problems by accompanying Galland. A direct man and a patriot, he was an admirer of Hitler and at the same time one of his sharpest critics.

After a thorough inspection of the two aerodromes and installations, the two generals settled down to a discussion with Nowotny and some of the more veteran pilots, including Wegmann, Schall, Preusker and Schnörrer, on flying the Me 262 operationally. Particular interest was shown in the dangers at take-off and landing. Keller wanted to know about dedication and fighting spirit, especially among the younger pilots. Nowotny invited Schnörrer to open the debate.

Quax, who had lost many friends in aerial battles, described the difference between a calculated attack and one made in blind passion. He knew the capabilities of the various fighters and their little idiosyncrasies and advanced the view that the maturity of an aircraft for battle was a precondition for success. Hitler had used exactly the same terms to Johannes Steinhoff as his justification for denying the jet to the fighter arm. Admitting it might be an eccentricity of his, Schnörrer observed nevertheless that in his opinion trust in the machine was essential for the fighting spirit of the pilot. After that he listed the known deficiencies of the Me 262 which remained uncorrected and which – as he knew – could not be remedied overnight.

All the pilots gathered in the group conceded privately that what Schnörrer had expressed was correct, but it was naturally also a question of personal mentality. Schnörrer's considerations about the maturity of an aircraft were utterly incomprehensible to fighter pilots who trusted to luck. To them, the important factor was that the 'power-house' should be fast and well-armed, and the rest could look after itself. Among fighter pilots there were all levels of mental approach to these matters.

One pilot would fly by the seat of his pants while another could not rest easy until he had triangulated his course on a chart allowing for all known vagaries of the wind between points A and B. Keller took a middle course, whatever that was, and considered Schnörrer too cautious. Thus his reaction was sceptical. History, he concluded, gave enough examples where fighting spirit and courage had been more decisive than the keenness of the sword. But Keller was unaware of the extent of Quax's experience. Schnörrer saw that he had said too much and fell silent. The conversation dried up for a spell and then re-opened along another avenue. Whether the tragic events of the following day were attributable to this conversation is an open question.

On the early morning of 8 November 1944 – Galland states 8 October in his book, but this is definitely an error – Galland, Keller, Nowotny and other officers of the Kommando Nowotny met at the Bramsche control centre for a short conference. The sun had still not risen when the radar post reported large concentrations of enemy bombers crossing the Zuider Zee. Another formation was over the Channel.

There are several versions of subsequent events. When enemy fighters were reported preceding the bombers, four Me 262s were ordered to intercept – Wegmann and Feldwebel Baudach from Achmer and Schall's two machines from Hesepe. While conventional Fw 190 fighters circled the two airfields, the latter aircraft got away first, as Wegmann's machines were still in the repair hangar and had to be towed out, thus delaying the procedure slightly. The battle began with the harsh staccato of flak from batteries distributed around both German airfields.

Initially all seemed to go well. Leutnant Schall was first to report in: 'Indians [slang for 'enemy'] in sight, I am attacking,' he said laconically. On the ground the observers all wore headphones through which the aerial fight could be followed. Leutnant Schall:

'We've knocked down one.' A few minutes later came Wegmann's report: 'We are in contact with the enemy,' and then briefly: 'I have shot down a Mustang.' Transmission ceased for a while. The silence was interrupted by more shooting. Leutnant Schall: 'My wingman has been shot down. I saw the aircraft crash in flames.' Outside the small hotel on the Bramsche road housing Preusker's radar centre the group searched the sky. Cloud cover was only five-tenths but nothing could be seen. Schall: 'My machine is on fire, I'm baling out.' Two enemy planes shot down for the price of two Me 262s!

Karl Schnörrer cast his eyes over the group which had Nowotny, Galland and Keller at its centre. Nowotny's face showed anger and bitter disappointment. Suddenly he turned to his driver standing beside Schnörrer and said, 'Come on, Gadecke, drive me to Achmer. You too, Quax, I'm going up.' Seconds later he was in the passenger seat of his BMW and ignored General Galland's command, 'Stay here, Nowotny!'

Schnörrer slipped into the back seat. He would have liked nothing better than to fly as Nowotny's wingman as he had done on more than 250 occasions on the Russian front but his knees were still in plaster from his last crash and for that reason he had not been trained for the Me 262.

At Achmer airfield Wegmann had landed. He could have flown alongside Nowotny but his aircraft had been shot at and went directly into the workshops. A pilot at Hesepe field – this must have been Schall – received orders to rendezvous with Nowotny in the air. Therefore the commander took off alone.

As Gadecke and Schnörrer arrived back at the control centre another bomber mass and its fighter escort was passing overhead. The bombers were occasionally visible through broken cloud, each four-engined bomber a black speck trailing a long silver stream. The earlier formation had already bombed and was heading for home.

The radio crackled and they heard Nowotny's calm voice. 'I am attacking.' There followed some bursts of fire and dull thumps, followed by a long period when he was concentrating on the job in hand and made no contact. Suddenly his voice was heard, rapid and alarmed. 'Shit, shit, my turbine.'

Schnörrer stared at the sky as if he could help him. 'Jump,

Walter,' he whispered repeatedly. He knew from Russia that his commander preferred to attempt the most dangerous landings with the undercarriage retracted rather than use his parachute. Perhaps Nowotny was worried about the Mustangs over the airfield – the incident involving Schall was still fresh in his mind. Actually there was no need to shoot at the pilot hanging from his parachute straps – the dirty deed could be done by flying just above the canopy and then climbing quickly: the silk would deflate in the propeller slipstream.

Nowotny made a last transmission: 'I have just shot down my third… left engine is out… I am being attacked… I have been hit…' The rest of what he said was garbled. On the ground the onlookers' anxious wait came to an end as suddenly the whistling noise typical of an Me 262 became audible and a jet shot out from the clouds, approaching and clearly shedding height. Just at that moment the sun broke through and glinted on a group of Mustang fighters falling towards the German aircraft in an almost vertical dive. There were several bursts of fire. Nobody gave the jet a chance. It was barely a few hundred metres up and would be an easy kill when it came in to land.

The Me 262 curved into an ever steeper incline and disappeared from sight. A few seconds later in the distance there was a dull thud. No fire, no mushroom cloud of smoke. All over. Nobody could accept it. 'Perhaps it wasn't Nowotny, perhaps it was Schall?' a voice suggested. Schnörrer moved up to the General der Jagdflieger. 'That was Nowotny, Herr General.'

'No!' Galland shouted. As the General jerked round, Quax saw that his face was graven in stone. Perhaps he was hoping against hope that it was somebody else. But even Galland couldn't make crashes unhappen.

'I am sorry General, but yes, it was him,' Schnörrer replied. In tears he turned away abruptly and joined Hauptmann Werner Wenzel in Nowotny's car. They drove off immediately for the crash site, the others following in their official vehicles. The small convoy stopped once or twice to check that they were heading in the right direction and eventually found the location on the edge of a wood near the small village of Epe close to Bramsche. The local fire brigade and an ambulance had got there very quickly but found a scene of utter devastation. There had been no explosion or fire, just an eerie stillness around the deep crater from which jutted bizarre scraps of the aircraft. Walter Nowotny was gone without a trace.

For Karl Schnörrer, Günther Wegmann and other pilots of the Kommando the self-questioning began. Why had Nowotny taken off against Galland's order? To what extent had his dreams and the assertions of General Keller affected his judgement? Schall seems to have been the pilot ordered to fly as Nowotny's wingman – had he made the rendezvous in the air? It seems doubtful. Therefore had Nowotny attacked alone? Was he trying to land the jet on one engine? Did the controls fail or was the Mustang attack the fatal event? Nowotny was still alive in the last phase of the dive and had probably tried to bale out at the last moment, for his half-opened and torn parachute pack was found near the crater. But what actually happened really remains something of a mystery.

Kommando Nowotny did not survive the death of its commander long. It existed from 1 October to 12 November 1944. Of the thirty aircraft supplied to the unit during that period, four were still airworthy on the last day. Twenty-six had been lost through enemy action or accident. The Kommando achieved between twenty-two and twenty-six victories. Thus the ratio of victories and losses was 1:1, an unsatisfactory situation in view of the superior speed of the jet. The delay before the Me 262 fighter was at last thrust into the front line lasted many months. This led – for reasons which are easily understandable – to a hasty, ill-considered and improvised state of operational readiness. In effect, the premiere was staged before the rehearsal and this moreover after a far too short period of normal working-up. In view of the war situation, time could not be spared either for a thorough training or to gain experience with the machine. 'The bird eats or dies' was now the byword, and there was precious little choice. That applied not only to the Me 262 units but also the Me 163s, the *Wilde Sau* night-fighters or the ramming Kommandos. Everything was in short supply: experienced pilots, instructors, fuel, safe transport. One thing which did still function was propaganda. Many clung to it, fearing the truth. The war had long passed the point where it might have still been possible to throw in the towel to avoid the final cruel act. Unconditional surrender was the only term on offer: total war demanded total defeat.

The figures are sobering. Between 1940 and 1945 nearly two million tons of bombs were dropped on Germany and the occupied territories. The Luftwaffe dropped 74,000 tons of bombs on England, about 3.7% of that amount. The number of dead after the raid on Hamburg alone was estimated at 60,000, equal to the total killed by bombing in all Great Britain throughout the war. The RAF dropped 700,000 tons of bombs on Germany and its aircraft flew 400,000 missions. Between 1939 and 1945, the Reich lost 72,000 military aircraft of all kinds.

The missions flown by Kommando Nowotny exhausted its strength within six short weeks. The grounds were only too obvious: the numerical superiority of the enemy fighter force made the siting of airfields close to the front, such as Achmer and Hesepe, imprudent. For enemy fighters it was no more than a cat's leap to keep close watch on these airfields every day and no greater risk than normal to attack jet aircraft taking off and landing there.

The majority of German fighter pilots were not yet 'at home' with the control stick as they were with the Me 109, Me 110 or Fw 190 and, since there was no basic combat training, not a few had their first taste of action after having flown the jet on only two or three occasions.

The Me 262 was not difficult to fly. This was an advantage on a peaceful training circuit but could create overconfidence. Kommando Thierfelder served primarily for pre-operational working up. Errors were generally forgiven by the aircraft. Kommando Nowotny was exclusively for operations. Under combat conditions it was suddenly very different. A careless turn, a high-speed pursuit after an enemy in a dive, a too-hasty shove at the throttle lever, forgetting absent-mindedly how long one had spent in the air: all these could have nasty or perhaps fatal consequences.

General Galland's order for a transfer back to Lechfeld for a battle pause, retraining and refitting came a few days after Nowotny's death. After looking over Achmer and Hesepe, Fritz Wendel reported:

The Loss of Nowotny

Kommando Nowotny was ordered back to Lechfeld for pilots and ground crew to retrain following the four losses of 8 November. This was on General Galland's order. I had already spoken personally on the weaknesses and faults of this Kommando at its formation. The pilots were only partially trained for fighter missions and thrown into action after only two training flights with the Me 262. Nothing had improved up to the time of Major Nowotny's death, which is now succeeded by General Galland ordering a period of further working up at Lechfeld. The Kommando needs eight to ten days to achieve full battle strength...

At Lechfeld, Major Erich Hohagen, an experienced fighter pilot, took over as Nowotny's successor. Wegmann remained as adjutant. By mid-December 1944 new aircraft had been flown in and flight-tested and a new draft of pilots afforded conversion training and a short technical course. By then Galland had specified as future operational bases the aerodromes at Brandenburg-Briest, Parchim and Oranienburg – all on the outskirts of Berlin. Kommando Nowotny was renamed JG7. Major Hohagen was named commander of III/JG7. Groups I and II were formed at Neumünster. Oberst Steinhoff, who had been involved with the Reich air defences with his old squadron since the retreats from North Africa and Italy, was appointed JG7 commodore.

More precious weeks were lost to unproductive maintenance or the laborious construction of ground installations. After Hohagen's III/JG7 had been transferred, the major delays were the time-consuming rail deliveries of aircraft and equipment from Lechfeld, Schwäbisch Hall or even Leipheim. The trains were under perpetual threat of attack from low-flying enemy aircraft throughout the day. Whence the order came that new aircraft should be delivered by train cannot be established. It meant that aircraft which had been flown to one of the three airfields had to be dismantled for transport by rail, this being a 500-kilometre journey at the mercy of enemy fighters which roamed at low level virtually unopposed. The actual figure of Me 262s destroyed while being transported by rail is not known. Those that arrived unscathed had then to be reassembled and flight tested again. Messerschmitt AG built an assembly hangar with all the necessary equipment at Brandenburg-Briest, but this was all much slower than having the aircraft ferried in by air. Messerschmitt's chief test pilot, Fritz Wendel, was in charge of flight-testing at Brandenburg-Briest and provided the official explanation for the long drawn-out transport operation and duplicated flight testing. Since there were insufficient pilots available to ferry the completed machines from assembly hangar to operational bases, the task would have fallen to operational pilots, thus depriving their squadrons of manpower. These hops from place to place were not without their attendant dangers from enemy fighters and it was considered preferable on the whole to transfer the jets by rail at night. There was undoubtedly some wisdom in this decision, for ferry pilots had only the briefest conversion course before climbing into the cockpit of an Me 262, and losses of aircraft through pilot error were high. All the same, to the operational pilots of JG7 twiddling their thumbs in the mess there was no sense in the order, for even a delivery flight enabled more experience of the aircraft to be gained, and if it were armed, enemy fighters could be engaged should they appear.

Meanwhile the 8th and 9th Squadrons of Nowotny's Kommando had been attached to III/JG7. 8th Squadron, under Leutnant Schall, operated from Oranienburg, while 9th Squadron was transferred to Parchim under the leadership of Hauptmann Georg Eder, a young and successful fighter pilot. Erich Hohagen remained at Brandenburg-Briest with the Group Staff.

At this time there was some disquiet in Allied circles concerning the Me 262 story. We know today that the much-delayed debut of the Me 262 jet fighter was something of a nightmare to our Western opponents and for the following reasons. The advance of Allied ground forces following the Normandy landings tied down a large part of their aerial forces. In December 1944 the Ardennes Offensive took the Americans very much by surprise, and in general their bomber offensive was not achieving the effect which had been expected of it. Furthermore some doubts were harboured regarding the ability of the Russians to press on to final success – or perhaps it was the case that this Soviet victory was not really wanted deep down.

The Loss of Nowotny

General Galland stated in his book that at a conference in Versailles on 11 January 1945 the Allied air chiefs were discussing the possibility of a longer duration to the war than hitherto. The obvious step-up in German fighter-aircraft production was the cause, and General Spaatz repeated personally his concerns about the Me 262 jet whose numbers were now estimated at about 700 (Galland put the figure at 564 completed aircraft at the end of 1944).

It seems likely that neither Spaatz nor his colleagues had knowledge of the various difficulties obstructing the deployment of the jet as a fighter, otherwise they might have had fewer worries. If their intelligence services did have wind of the altercations between Hitler and the Luftwaffe High Command, however, the disconcerting successes almost daily of such fighter jets as were operational must have given them food for thought. A speed of from 300 to 400 kph in excess of the best Allied piston-engined fighters was not the only shock. Despite the defeats in the south, and the pincers squeezing them between west and east, the Luftwaffe was still able to maintain a high level of operational readiness among its pilots, and its fighters remained a potent force.

10

Rudi Sinner and III/JG7 – Best of All German Jet-fighter Units

I n a letter to the author dated 26 January 1977, Adolf Galland stated that when the Kommando Nowotny had been reformed into III/JG7, it became the best of all the jet-fighter units. Rudolf Sinner was commander of III/JG7 from its inception until 4 April 1945 when his Luftwaffe flying career came to an abrupt end.

During the opening phase of the Normandy landings, Hauptmann Rudolf Sinner was commander of I/JG27. His mission was to lead his Group flying Me 109s to an operational area south of Caen, and he had taken off from Vertus airfield near Epernay in Champagne. Once in the air he discovered that his guns were unserviceable and in the confusion of the first dogfights a short while later turned for home since he was unable to take part in the fighting. In the skies over Normandy 200 German machines were pitted against 5,000 Allied fighters. Sinner's return to Epernay was a race against death. In his earphones one warning of enemy fighters groups followed another. He had barely escaped a clutch of Lightnings over Paris when his engine began to stutter at 18,000 feet. Then Vertus airfield reported enemy fighters circling overhead. It was a ticklish situation, but Sinner had known worse. If the spluttering motor did not die altogether, so he calculated, from this height he could get his aircraft down in about fifteen minutes. If the enemy fighters were still there, he would be forced to make a crash-landing somewhere nearby. Feverishly he searched all points of the heavens, suddenly made out high above him four – no six –

USAAF Thunderbolts. They came for him, and a few seconds later a bullet shredded his reflecting gunsight. Defenceless, he threw back his cabin hood, tore open the clasp of his seat straps and jumped. He let himself fall freely, struggling to focus on the terrain below, made out the great stretches of vineyards and hills of the Champagne district. At once he recalled the upright pointed wooden stakes which supported the vines. To be impaled on one was not something he wished to experience. Another ground feature worth avoiding near Epernay were the defensive fortifications from World War I garnished with barbed wire. These positions were protected by upright iron stakes embedded in concrete. Once Sinner had identified, as he believed, a large field of low wine-stocks devoid of stakes, he pulled the rip cord of his parachute, and with canopy deployed swept towards this field which was skirted by a broad avenue. Drifting in, he was rotated until his back was to the wind, hit the ground violently, stumbled, struck the back of his head against a low boundary wall and lost consciousness.

When he came to a few minutes later, he found a number of men dressed in blue overalls crouching or standing over him, each with a knife at hand. Sinner took fright for a moment at the threatening scene, and then his mind cleared and he realised that the men were harmless viticulturists – field workers. They took care of him, one man cleaning the oil patches from his uniform jacket and trousers. The oil told him that besides the gunsight, the engine had been hit – he had had a lucky escape. A few moments later an elderly, white-haired, well-dressed man appeared and to Sinner's surprise addressed him in fairly good German. He had watched the chase from the window of his house, seen the German aircraft shot down and the parachute appear. A horse-drawn waggon was summoned and Sinner was taken to an apartment in the nearby Abbois Chateau from where Sinner's Group at Vertus was informed by telephone. While awaiting transport, M. Durant explained that he had been an officer in the Great War and was now a representative of the Mercier champagne firm. He was quite open about his support for the Germans and how he viewed with misgivings the Allied landings.

Once in Vertus, the Group surgeon ordered Sinner four weeks' bedrest. Sinner ignored his advice and, since he felt fine next day, was soon up and about. Forty-eight hours later he was circling the airfield in a Fieseler Storch to make sure he was fit to resume flying but experienced a giddy spell while coming in to land and had to put the aircraft down on the nearest patch of grass. Very severe headaches developed rapidly and now he accepted medical advice, put himself to bed and was flown a short while later to Munich and then Bad Wiessee where he needed a month or so of convalescence.

Immediately he was declared fit for duty a telephone call came from General Galland's office at Berlin-Gatow ordering Sinner to report there two days later. Upon arrival in due course he met his former JG27 commodore, Oberst Edu Neumann, Galland's ADC. That evening Neumann, Sinner and Hannes Trautloft, Inspector of Day-fighters, dined in the officers' mess. First Neumann informed Sinner that he had been promoted to Major, after which Galland and his future successor, Oberst Gollob, joined the party and in the cinema watched a film showing the Me 163 rocket fighter under test. The machine had just become operational, and immediately upon seeing this aircraft – faster than the Me 262 – climb, bank and land, Sinner volunteered to fly it. Gollob laughed and told him, 'She's not for you, Sinner, you would have to learn how to glide then take a complete conversion course, and we don't have the time. Nor do you. I'll make you another suggestion – how do you feel about the Me 262?' He gave Sinner a shrewd look before continuing, 'That should suit you, and you could write up a whole host of Defect Reports about it to help us.' This was a sly dig at Sinner's way of getting matters put to rights – get it down on paper. Like Gollob, he was Austrian, but not the cinema stereotype – though sociable, and fond of a glass of wine, as a soldier he put the Prussians in the shade. Not by military posture or clever dialectic – his Austrian brogue was far too thick for that – but in contrast to many he was a soldier first and then an airman. A stickler for detail, he was never prepared to accept second best, nor tolerate anything that failed to work the way it should have done. If he discovered anywhere the opportunity to improve something or even the slightest negligence, then Sinner reported it in a more or less comprehensive Defect Report. His personal combat readiness after one hundred aerial engagements remained as much above reproach as his interpretation of a soldier's duty.

Reflecting on the Me 163, he saw fairly swiftly that this manned, rocket-propelled glider, although endowed with phenomenal speed and rate of climb, was of very limited tactical value on account of its short flight time. Little could be achieved in the maximum of ten minutes before the fuel was expended. The short radius of action offered nothing useful to a flier to whom the endurance of the Me 109 was insufficient. All the more was he attracted by the offer that he should undergo conversion training to the Me 262 at Lechfeld and then join JG7. He had never flown the aircraft, but what he had heard of its merits impressed him. At Landsberg he had needed only two days' conversion from the Me 109 to the Me 110, for he found that there was little difference between single- and twin-engined aircraft.

At Lechfeld in August 1944 the Thierfelder Kommando was responsible for Me 262 pilot training. After his first look round, what Major Sinner observed did not please him in the least. He had almost five years' front-line airfield experience. His watchwords were 'Preparation and Operational Readiness'. The way they ran Lechfeld reminded him of the peaceful Thirties. Each morning the aircraft were towed slowly to the runway and eventually flown off. On their return, if work needed to be done on the machines, there would be long discussions before the aircraft were brought to shelter. What amazed him most was the MYO procedure. 'MYO' was wireless telegraphy (W/T) jargon for 'Enemy Aircraft Approaching' and was given as a preliminary warning so that all machines could be brought to protected positions. It was the rule at Lechfeld aerodrome that when the MYO alert was broadcast, all aircraft – particularly the highly valued Me 262 jets – were towed to camouflaged areas hidden from the enemy's view. It was an obvious safety measure at all schools which had no operational fighter pilots.

Sinner took up this point with Leutnant Müller whom he knew and who was, like himself, an experienced fighter pilot. In conversation he learned that few, if any, of the pilots being Me 262 trained at Lechfeld were from the fighter arm. Müller confirmed that they were almost exclusively naval air arm, bomber and transport pilots from all regions. Yesterday, even an NCO bomber pilot with the Knight's Cross, Oberfeldwebel Buchner, had arrived, he confided. Leutnant Müller was beside himself with almost mutinous rage. They ran Lechfeld like a civilian flying club. Until yesterday when a stop had finally been put to the practice, every pilot passing out from conversion training had been the bashful recipient of a bouquet of roses. On the credit side, however, Müller could report that the actual training in Oberleutnant Wörner's squadron was of an excellent standard, and even the odd operation had been flown, once or twice with a success at the end of it. Sinner was able to confirm Wörner's good reputation when he embarked upon his own jet training course. His first flight passed off without difficulties, he experienced the Me 262 soft-as-a-peach-hanging-in-the-air sensation after take-off and the joy of the aircraft's speed at higher altitudes. Landings were no problem.

—⁓—

Upon terminating his training successfully Sinner asked Oberleutnant Wörner if any operational experience was planned as a supplement and also if any radio direction post had ever been set up to monitor time in flight and Me 262 characteristics. Most of all he wanted to know if statistics were being kept regarding minimum and maximum endurance at various altitudes. Wörner replied that as good as nothing had been done in that area and apart from the few experiences gained by Thierfelder and his first team of pilots no records kept. On hearing this, Sinner conferred with Leutnant Müller and Oberfeldwebel Buchner regarding the possibility of joint operational exercises. He had discovered on the perimeter of the Lechfeld aerodrome a night-fighter radio direction post equipped with a small Seeburg radar set, discussed a working collaboration with the ground officers and begged Wörner for two jets to try out his plan. Wörner declined with regret, since he was himself short of the requirement. Sinner rang Nowotny at Achmer, explained his idea and a short while later two Me 262s were transferred in.

Sinner's improvised operation was successful. On the first trial he operated the Seeburg himself while Leutnant Müller went up to intercept a solo-flying reconnaissance Mosquito reported on course approaching Munich. Müller was homed in on the Allied aircraft by radar, came up behind the RAF machine over the city and claimed a kill after hitting the enemy with a burst of fire and watching it disappear into cloud below. It was later known that the Mosquito landed at an Allied base in Italy on one engine, but at least the pilot had been prevented from fulfilling his mission.

On the second operation, Oberfeldwebel Buchner pursued a French-piloted Spitfire to Stuttgart and obtained a kill over the city outskirts. Sinner took the jet up himself for the third trial and headed for a pair of four-engined bombers identified on radar. He had obtained a fighter direction officer from the Fighter Division as his controller and provided him with the most detailed schedules about Me 262s flight timings and other particulars. Unfortunately Sinner and his controller were both conscientious types, and this contributed to the failure of the operation. Sinner had been directed successfully into a position directly astern of the two Allied bombers at 6,000 feet. As soon as he had visual contact he released the safety-catch of his machine-guns and – as the distance to the enemy machines closed steadily – aimed. The range was still too great for a certain hit, but the 'Indians' were flying such a nice straight course direct for Berlin that it seemed to Sinner that all aboard bar the pilot must have been taking a siesta. All at once he received in his headphones the controller's order: 'Break off attack immediately and return to Garden Hedge!' Sinner could scarcely believe his ears and responded that he was on the point of attacking. The controller was adamant: 'Return immediately!' Sinner had no means of knowing the reasons the controller had for issuing this strict order, and in a rage he broke off the attack, looked left and right, made a long turn suspecting the possibility of an attack from below had been identified on radar. The sky was empty. After landing he learned that the controller – untrained in Me 262 direction – had adhered strictly to the flying-time schedule, the inflexibility of which Sinner had impressed upon him in the usual terms. Thus the two bombers had been spared by a matter of seconds.

It is a rarity to find, among all the thousands of aerial engagements which took place during the Second World War, the respective contact reports of two opposing pilots. At around noon on 26 November 1944, Rudi Sinner took off from Lechfeld in an Me 262 fighter jet following the report of four Lightnings approaching Munich. At the controls of one of these four aircraft, a so-called 'Long-nose Lightning' (so-called by the Germans because the forward part of the fuselage had been elongated to accommodate reconnaissance cameras) was USAAF Lieutenant Renne. The other three Lightnings were standard-design flying fighter-cover for the reconnaissance machine. The reports of Sinner and Renne can be matched as follows:

Renne: It was my mission to photograph the rail marshalling yards at Munich. I had taken off from San Severo in Italy with fighter escort, had completed the task and was just turning for home when I saw about 500 feet below and ahead of me the silhouette of an Me 262. As it started to climb towards me I radioed a message to the fighter escort requesting assistance. As I did this, I watched the faster Me 262 get above me in a turning manoeuvre and set himself on my tail.

Sinner: After taking off from Lechfeld I climbed as quickly as possible and headed for Munich on a converging course with the contact. Suddenly I saw the Long-nose Lightning above me flying in the opposite direction. I was intending to attack out of the sun, but because of our relative heights this was not possible and so I made a long climbing turn to get on the enemy's tail.

Renne: I discarded my supplementary fuel tanks, gave full throttle and banked as tightly as possible in the attempt to get to grips with my opponent. He fired his first burst when we were at the same altitude and on a collision course.

Sinner: Initially I was not able to get into a good shooting position because the enemy aircraft made a very long drawn-out turn. The 'Indian' saved himself banking steeply to the right, I could not follow because the radius was too tight for my jet. I put both engines to maximum throttle but even then I failed to get the target in my sights. By now one of the escort fighters had appeared. He appeared hesitant and this allowed me to get in close to him. At the last moment he cut his speed back and made a clever turn-away to get clear. My immediate reaction was to attempt a tighter turn while climbing under reduced throttle but this did not achieve the required effect. During this manoeuvring duel the Long-nose had put distance between us, and I saw the other two escort fighters turning towards me from the north east. I had reduced my speed substantially and made a turn of large radius, and believing that the two Lightning fighters would now attack I decided to refuse combat and dive. I was hoping to catch up with the Long-nose during the dive, but it was so steep that my speed was soon approaching Mach 1 and I had to pull out at once. I watched the Lightnings regroup and turn towards the south.

Renne: After the Me 262 fired his burst, I went into a steep dive to the right, saw my opponent flying a wide semi-circular course and received instructions from the fighter escort to make a left turn and leave the bandit to them. I did this and made contact with the escort which had not been able to get at the Me. I lost them to sight in a cloudbank and as they were anxious to return for shortage of fuel, we grouped up for this purpose.

Sinner: I lost contact with the Lightnings for a short while by flying through cloud. Up to that time I had never been in a favourable shooting position and had not fired. [Leutnant Renne must therefore have mistaken the reflection of the sun against the perspex canopy of the German jet for machine-gun fire as Renne flew on a collision course with the sun at his back towards Sinner.] Despite my low fuel reserve I turned towards the enemy group at full throttle. Their condensation trails were easy to make out. After about twelve minutes' pursuit I caught up with the four Lightnings. They were not flying in any kind of formation and I aimed for the two inner machines in the hope of hitting whichever was the Long-nose. I got a hit instead on the escort fighter flown by Lieutenant Julius Thomas.

Renne: We were flying south and were almost over the Alps (he probably means the Hohe Tauern mountain range south of Kitzbühel. *Translator's note*) when we noticed a pursuing Me 262 which was closing fast. The escort banked to engage while I maintained a southerly heading to get the films home. When the fighter rejoined me, I saw that the machine piloted by Lieutenant Thomas was missing. The Me 262 had followed Thomas down.

Sinner: I saw that my fire had hit the tailplane and right wing of the enemy machine and as he fell away in a steep dive I made a sort of angled dive to the left to follow. During this man-oeuvre I overtook the disabled enemy but then abandoned the chase for shortage of fuel. I learned later that Lieutenant Thomas had baled out and landed safely on a slope of the Füllsteinhorn near Kitzbühel where he was taken prisoner by the mountain guard squad.

Following this successful encounter under the directions of the same controller who had nipped in the bud the earlier chase after the two Berlin-bound bombers, ruffled feathers were smoothed and the two officers now enjoyed a better working relationship. Sinner made it home safely on his last drop of spirit, while the radar officer learned the lesson that second rate was sometimes better than first when it came to interpreting Sinner's orders.

Despite his success against the Lightnings, Sinner had not forgotten the escape of the two bombers. He had now switched his priority to attacking heavy bombers on air-raid missions but found himself without his jets. The two borrowed Me 262s had had to be returned to JG7, to where he was himself transferred after Nowotny's death.

Rudi Sinner and III/JG7

The conditions he discovered at Brandenburg-Briest were worse than at Lechfeld. There were few aircraft, the weather was miserable and operational flying was not generally possible. Nobody knew when the first jet aircraft would arrive and in what numbers. 'Loafing' was writ in larger letters here than at Lechfeld, where at least the flight training courses had been functioning, and at Brandenburg everyone did more or less as he pleased. Somebody hunted hares regularly, another cared for a kennel of greyhounds abandoned by their former owner for lack of food. There was a flourishing skat school and others rambled in the country. Most pilots – used to almost daily operational missions with their former units – hated nothing more than this inactivity, waiting in uncertainty for X-Day.

On his transfer Major Sinner had been given to understand that at Brandenburg-Briest, group and squadron commanders had already been appointed. Sinner would not have minded flying as a simple pilot without an office, but here there was simply no flying. It was little consolation to discover that Erich Hohagen and the others were no better off.

Thus it came as a relief to receive the summons from Gollob to attend a large Jägerstab conference in Berlin. The Jägerstab had been set up in early 1944 on the suggestion of Director Schaaf of the Speer ministry, established by Milch and approved by Hitler. Its purpose was to get the heavily damaged aircraft industry into bomb-proof factories, to rebuild and reverse the seriously impaired production figures. Head of the Jägerstab was Karl-Otto Saur, a fanatical Nazi, a civil servant employed at the Todt and Speer ministries whose energy and vision were excelled only by the lack of scruple he showed in forcing through his plans. In Holland he had been called 'the scourge of German industry'.

Upon entering the great hall, Sinner came face-to-face with at least 1,500 well-known personalities from heavy industry and armaments, among them a few military people and civil servants. The agenda was wide-ranging. Coal, locomotives, waggons, steel and much else was discussed before finally the question of Me 262 aircraft was reached. Speaking with reference to the subject heading 'Me 262 Supply', General Thomas from the Reich Air

Ministry opened with a few observations and was interrupted by Saur asking: 'What exactly is the problem here? I have been advised by industry that a large number of Me 262 aircraft are waiting to be removed from factories, that JG7 is the only squadron due to receive these machines and is complaining that they haven't got any.'

General Thomas indicated that a Major Sinner of JG7 was present and he could report on the state of affairs. Sinner stood to introduce himself and was commissioned at once by Saur to look into the difficulties which seemed to exist and to ensure they were removed. 'Drive or fly to southern Germany,' Saur said in conclusion, 'and get everything sorted out. You have plenipotentiary powers to take whatever measures are necessary. At the end of the conference you will have your instructions and authority in writing.'

That same night, Sinner took the night train to Augsburg to consult with Fritz Wendel. The latter brought up at once a gripe known to both. 'One of the main difficulties of flying in and out is the MYO rule. This rule states that it is absolutely forbidden to fly when MYO is in effect, and so our aircraft have to remain on the ground, and are towed away to safety. And that happens sometimes more than once a day.' Sinner explained the point of view he had often argued at Lechfeld that aircraft were safer in the air than on the ground and pointed to the many Me 262s destroyed on airfields. 'It is better,' he concluded, 'if you allow your ferry pilots to parachute out in a problem case rather than continually suspend delivery flights on the grounds of enemy operations which may come nowhere near the airfield. Moreover,' he added, 'at individual airfields one could operate an industry-protection non-jet fighter group to keep enemy fighters occupied while the Me 262s make their landings.'

Wendel suggested training ferry pilots in the fighter defensive role and referred Sinner to the ferry-pilot Kommando at Obertraubling. He had put out feelers there himself but had been unsuccessful.

At Obertraubling Sinner contacted an Oberleutnant responsible for the Kommando in question and who explained the great difficulties encountered in Me 262 delivery. There were endless

MYO warnings and every so often the meteorological office grounded aircraft because at this time of year the Thuringian forest often experienced cloud at ground level.

Sinner was enraged. 'Those are not plausible reasons,' he replied. 'There are all types of weather conditions, and it is not the meteorologist but your pilots who will decide in future whether they will fly or not after they have considered the overall situation. They can fly above the Thuringian forest because at 27,000 feet there is no cloud. You will send your best pilots to Lechfeld for Me 262 conversion training, and these will then deliver Me 262s to the operational airfields.'

After that he called on the meteorologist, scarcely believing his eyes when he saw the milk-glass windows which shielded any view of the outdoors. The duty meteorologist put up a defence. They had their instructions which had to be followed, and that was what they did, he argued with annoyance. Sinner produced his pleni-potentiary authority and said quietly: 'With all respect to your instructions, bombs fall in all weathers, and we need aircraft. As from today you will provide Me 262 ferry pilots with the current weather situation by telephone at take-off time and not supply old weather reports over which you have been deliberating for several hours. Then it is up to the ferry pilot if he will fly or not. If you refuse I am obliged to have you replaced.'

The threat was not made seriously, but it worked. The meteorologist, in civilian life a high-school teacher, went white in the face. In the gentlest Austrian dialect of which he was capable, Sinner said in parting: 'Look at it from our point of view, Herr Professor. We in the front line simply cannot say we're not fighting today because it's raining.' And with that he left.

At Augsburg Sinner resumed his discussions with Wendel about what steps still needed to be taken. Again he found himself much impressed by the expert technical knowledge and reliability of this famous Messerschmitt chief test pilot who never tried to shirk his responsibility and was always ready when needed. Sinner came to value him increasingly the longer he knew him.

Finally Sinner contacted the Fighter Division to ensure their co-operation and support for the arrangements, orders and measures he was about to take. By now it was Christmas 1944. He spent a sad and soulless holiday at Lechfeld, mostly alone in unheated rooms and houses unvisited by the least Christmas spirit. During the early hours the telephone rang. Oberst Hannes Trautloft announced himself and said: 'Sinner, something decisive has happened which I can't explain to you properly over the 'phone. Your commodore, Steinhoff, has been relieved of command with immediate effect. Galland and Hohagen have also gone. We have to patch up the gaps as quickly as possible. You have the choice of taking over JG300 or JG301 as commodore, or if you like, Hohagen's Group at Brandenburg-Briest.' When Sinner made no reply, Trautloft added, 'Reflect on it well, but I must have your decision soon.' Sinner answered at once: 'I don't need time to consider, Herr Oberst, I think I am well prepared to accept command of III/JG7.'

'Very good, Sinner,' Trautloft concluded, 'I thought you would probably decide that way. So, go now to Brandenburg-Briest and take over the Group. Everything else you will learn later. Until later then. That's all.'

11

III/JG7 – The Last Great Air-battle
over the Reich

A fresh breeze was already blowing through Brandenburg-Briest when Major Sinner assumed command of III/JG7. The new JG7 commodore, Major Weissenberger, was as determined as Sinner to make a mark, and both rolled up their sleeves for the job ahead. The first concern was aircraft. The success of Sinner's intervention in resolving the Me 262 supply problem was plain to see. Every day Weissenberger rang Berlin and Augsburg to keep the pot on the boil. Soon the forlorn aircraft park began to expand; Fritz Wendel was more often at Brandenburg than at Messerschmitt's to monitor the incoming deliveries and fly whenever the opportunity presented itself.

A major problem now as before was the armament of the Me 262. Despite the good success rate up to the present, it was clear that because of the much higher closing speed during attacks against enemy aircraft, the jet would be more effective with more modern weapons. On account of their limited scatter, the conventional machine-guns of the time required the shortest possible range, but close approach tactics brought a greater danger of being shot down or collision.

Hauptmann Schleicher of the Rechlin Test Centre heard of these problems in conversation and discussed with Major Christl, head of Weapons Testing Kommando 25 at Rechlin and Parchim how best to overcome them. Christl was running trials with an air-to-air rocket designated R4M developed jointly by Messerschmitt

AG and Rheinmetall Borsig. The battery consisted of twenty-four solid-fuel rockets weighing 3.85 kg each and fitted with a 520-gram HE warhead. A dozen would be rigged in a wooden firing rack slung below each wing. They were fired by depressing a button on the control column and the normal reflex gunsight was sufficient for aiming purposes. The great advantage of the R4M rocket was its great accuracy, substantially greater effect and, most importantly, that they could be fired from 1,500 metres, a much longer range than the standard machine-gun. Velocity of the rocket was 525 m/sec. This was exactly the thing required by Me 262 fighter pilots to maximise fully the speed advantage of their aircraft.

There was no time to lose, and this meant sidestepping bureau-cracy. Major Christl agreed to supply two rocket sets with racks. Oberst Gollob, Galland's replacement as General der Jagdflieger, gave the scheme his unofficial blessing without mentioning it to Goering. Friedrich Schwarz, to whom the Messerschmitt weapons division was directly answerable, sent his young representative Will Langhammer to Parchim and soon the first R4M-armed Me 262 fighter stood ready in the hangar.

Who would test-fly it? A number of volunteers presented them-selves, others warned against it, for there was no knowing how the aircraft would react to the extra loading. The apparatus with 100 kilos of rockets slung below the wings might easily cause a problem of aerodynamics and then who knew what might follow? It was agreed to seek the advice of Wendel, for he was ultimately responsible for all kinds of test flights. He came at once, looked over the machine, climbed in, taxied to the runway and took off. Upon landing he had no observations to make regarding influences affecting the flight characteristics of the jet and gave it the thumbs-up. The extra weight reduced the aircraft's speed by 5 kph, he said, but there was no reason why the jet should not fly with the rocket fitment. Subsequently he made two flights to nearby Müritzsee, fired a salvo while on an inclined dive and observed no irregular response by the machine.

The question now arose where the rack assembly for the remaining aircraft of the Group would come from. The weapon was not yet being mass-produced and there was no workshop or factory. Schwarz and Langhammer would provide the rockets but the wooden racks could not be turned out at Messerschmitt's.

Sinner and Wegmann decided to take matters into their own hands. After a brief search they enlisted the help of the Gauleiter of Schwerin and soon came across a large furniture factory prepared to make the racks on the existing drawings. A second carpentry firm volunteered to make the rails and retention assembly. In this simple manner two harmless woodworking businesses were transformed into an armaments-producing factory of a special kind.

The test flights were made at Parchim, where all of 9th Squadron had been fitted with the new equipment by 10 March 1945. General der Jagdflieger Oberst Gordon Gollob gave his approval without even consulting Goering. On 17 March, the new Inspecteur der Jagdflieger, Oberstleutnant Walther Dahl, Trautloft's successor, visited Parchim in order to watch a demonstration by an Me 262 using the new weaponry. The aircraft was piloted by Günther Wegmann, 9th Squadron commander. On the west side of the airfield was the burnt-out remains of an Italian Savoya transport aircraft. Diving in a light incline, Wegmann shot the wreck of the old machine into a thousand pieces from 1,000 metres. No more eloquent argument in favour of the new weapon could possibly have been made. And the final proof, if it were needed, came the very next day.

Just after five on the morning of 18 March 1945, a large bomber formation was reported to be assembling over London, its expected target Berlin. Wegmann's 262 had gone into the repair hangar the previous afternoon and was not operational and he accepted a substitute machine. Meanwhile 1,200 bombers escorted by fifty P-51 fighters were reported en route for Berlin.

Wegmann took off with a seven-strong squadron. Before the wave of bombers reached the Reich capital, the squadron made contact with the enemy. These were aircraft of US 457 Bomber Group. It was to be the last great air-battle of the European war, and the first in which air-to-air rockets were used operationally.

The German jets were flying in a loose, strung-out formation and made a wide banking approach to engage the heavily laden four-engined bombers. Wegmann picked out a formation consisting of about sixty enemy machines and signalled to attack. To his right was Oberleutnant Seeler, to his left Schnörrer with Oberfähnrich Windisch on the outside. They were at 6,000 metres when Wegmann fired salvoes from 1,000 metres. Within seconds the others had fired off their rockets too. The effect of 144 projectiles fired into the midst of a tight bomber formation was devastating. Flying above the melee in order to get clear of the enemy fighters, Wegmann saw only bits of aircraft, flame and smoke as he looked down. The remainder of his squadron had gone, dispersed to all points of the compass. He concentrated on the homeward flight, was given the course to steer by his controller and kept a close watch for enemy fighters. While doing this he spotted another formation of bombers and turned to attack with his machine-guns. There was a kind of agreement in force that two kills per flight per man was to be aimed for. He had definitely already destroyed one bomber, perhaps two; in the heat of battle it was difficult to see exactly. Now with a bit of luck he could score a definite second victory. As he came up on the new formation from astern, while still out of MK 108 range he selected the Flying Fortress on the right extremity of the wave and came in for the kill. At between 500 and 600 metres he opened fire, felt the typical hard jerks as the rapid stream of bullets left his guns, saw almost at once the cowling of one of the bomber's engines right side rip away. Jubilant he pressed the W/T transmit button to report his success, but at that moment a hail of fire hit his fighter forward. A heavy blow struck his right leg. Before his eyes the armoured windscreen splattered, the instruments fell from their sockets, and wherever he looked were bullet holes and rents. Then it fell quiet. He felt his leg. There was a numbness. He knew that something was wrong but at first he hoped it might have been just a hard blow from the control stick when it was hit, or from the foot pedals. He groped down the limb gingerly: just below the knee his fingers discovered a large, deep wound of about ten fingers' width. He found his hand covered with blood when he raised it. His first thought was: I have lost the leg. But he still felt no pain.

Wegmann's aircraft was at 6,000 metres. So far as he was able, he watched the skies for enemy fighters while weaving with irregular left and right turns. The enemy had gone, the bomber formation had moved on towards its target. His first thought was to bale out, but he was still too high to do so. To be used for firing practice while dangling from a parachute, especially as a jet pilot, was no longer a rarity in the increasing bitterness of this air-war. Leutnant Schall's experience had proved it.

Wegmann attempted to make a W/T transmission but the set was no longer working. He was chilled to the marrow: the cause was shock and probably loss of blood. It was another reason for the time being not to abandon his aircraft since he did not want to run the risk of hypothermia during the long descent. Thoughts chased through his mind in rapid succession. And then suddenly he became anxious.

He knew he had to shed height at all costs and headed for Parchim in a light dive in the hope of coming under the protection of the home fighter defence. He was controlling the engines by ear since all instruments had been shot to pieces. When he got to an altitude which he estimated at 4,000 metres, he noticed small flames stabbing from the starboard engine. The port turbine seemed intact. Now he had no choice, with a serious leg wound and one turbine aflame he could not risk a crash-landing. He still did not know if it would actually be possible to evacuate the machine, but the parachute was his only hope.

He was still too high and with time on his hands went through the procedure mentally. He had never baled out before and had only verbal desciptions of the procedure to go by. Throw the cabin hood off, force yourself from your seat, and leave the aircraft upwards, don't do a sideways roll. One could push the control stick forwards to be catapulted free by centrifugal force. Another method was to put the aircraft upside down and fall out. Since he tended by nature to follow the conventional path, Wegmann chose the first method despite the known danger of coming into contact with the tailplane.

He took off his flying helmet and throat microphone, raised his gloved hands and unfastened the clasp of the seat straps. He felt sick: the stink of raw fuel had penetrated the still-enclosed cockpit.

Just in time! he thought, and he removed the bolt securing the cabin hood, which whipped off immediately, and pushed up with his arms to get his head above the leading edge of the windscreen. A fraction of a second later the maelstrom sucked him from the cockpit at 350 kph. He bounced against the tailplane on his un-injured left side but got free unscathed. He counted five long seconds before pulling the release cord of his pilot 'chute to ensure he did not fall into the path of the hurtling machine, or allow the canopy to become ensnared in the airframe.

He drifted slowly to earth. There was plenty of time to consider his strategy of how to land with a serious leg wound. Would his good leg alone be able to withstand the impact? When he was low enough to estimate his approximate touch-down point, he recognised the town of Wittenberge which he knew well, having overflown it on many occasions. He still scanned the skies for enemy fighters, but apparently they had gone off with the bombers to the target.

He had drifted beyond Wittenberge, was only a few hundred metres up and was gliding towards a wood extending to the edge of a small village. He had to pray that he would skirt the tall trees, there was nothing he could do to avoid them. Luck was with him. He was just high enough to brush the tree tops with his feet before sinking towards a clearing among the pines adjoining a meadow. With his good leg leading he powered into the trunks of the saplings, toppled into a depression on his injured side while the canopy spilled into the meadow. He felt no pain. The wounded leg was as dead as if it were anaesthetised.

The first person to reach him across the meadow was an elderly woman. 'German pilot!' he cried to her, for he was wearing, as many German airmen did then, an American leather flying jacket with fur collar which bore across the shoulders in yellow characters the unit of its original owner. Wegmann had obtained the garment from a shot-down American flier. It sometimes happened now-adays that German civilians, hardened and vengeful over the devastation of their cities and the terrible casualties, took the law into their own hands when capturing Allied bomber crews. Günther Wegmann had no wish to become the victim of a fatal misunderstanding on account of his fur-collared jacket. Less than a hundred metres behind the woman several men were running across the meadow towards him

The woman had been a nursing sister and knew how to apply emergency first aid. She bound the thigh above the right knee and applied a tourniquet before making Wegmann comfortable in the grass. She then sent one of the men to the nearby village of Glöwen to summon an ambulance from the hospital at Wittenberge.

'Four hours later my leg was off,' Wegmann wrote in conclusion to his combat report.

In this last great air-battle in Europe of the Second World War, the Allied air forces lost 41 four-engined bombers and five fighters before reaching their target, Berlin. 16 bombers were hit by flak over the approaches to the city and either crashed or – seriously damaged – made emergency landings behind the Russian lines. 9th Squadron III/JG7 destroyed 25 bombers for the loss of Oberleutnant Karl-Heinz Seeler, who had attacked on Wegmann's right and was shot down by B-17s west of Perleberg, and the two aircraft.

12

Last Gestures of Defiance

T he months of March and April 1945 drew the war pitilessly towards its conclusion. Endless streams of refugees from the eastern provinces of the Reich made their way westwards almost shoulder-to-shoulder with Stalin's advancing divisions. Penetrating ever deeper into Germany from the West, not quite so impetuously but still conscious of approaching victory, were the Americans, British and French. For German forces there was really no point in fighting on, in dying for the cause: it served no useful purpose to offer further resistance, but yet they did. They fought on, not knowing why, defending a Reich that no longer existed. They defended it on land, at sea and in the air, as soldiers always have. The air was full of bullets, shrapnel and splinters as was the ground, but it was more dangerous in the air because things happened faster and gave you no time to reflect.

Enemy fighters roamed as if in peacetime the skies of the land they had been taught to hate. Rarely did they come up against opposition. Enemy bombers dropped their bombs, and carried on the killing while the fighters machine-gunned any useful target that presented itself. The nation below them had forfeited its right to live. Kill them then!

The months of March and April 1945 were the hardest in the short career of the Me 262, those crowned with the greatest success and mourned for the most losses. III/JG7 was now joined by Jagdverband 44, whose brief existence will be described towards the end of this chapter. JV44 was commanded by Adolf Galland, deposed General der Jagdflieger.

Wherever the gaze fell in Germany, in whatever province, something could be seen exploding, burning or smouldering. Military order within a Luftwaffe squadron or group community was no longer possible. The enemy dictated the course of events. Supply, maintenance, repair, the number of operational machines, training, trials, delivery flights – over them all hovered the need to improvise, and this was successful if the hour favoured the undertaking.

The men and women of the communications networks and the ground-crew Spartans achieved the nigh-impossible, at work day and night in the hangars, hardly able to keep their eyes open for lack of sleep, their only opportunity for rest was when collapsed in a bunker or slit trench at the approach of enemy aircraft. And whenever a pilot, whose machine or weapons they had overhauled the previous day, failed to return, in a sense they shared in the loss. And right up to the last day, no pilot had to be asked twice to fly a mission.

The story of the Me 262 in March and April 1945 is written in the sky in blood. One dramatic air-battle followed another. Bombers exploded while the jet's armoured windscreen splintered. A *Rotte* [flying formation consisting of a pair], or four, or six Me 262s would venture into the field of defensive fire of a swarm of ten to fifteen four-engined bombers whose tail-gunners would keep firing as long as the finger could be crooked around a trigger.

Almost daily III/JG7 received a warning of bombers approaching. One day, four jets rose to intercept, one *Rotte* led by Georg Eder, the other by Quax Schnörrer. Eder was an old war-horse: seventy-eight victories in the West by the war's end, twelve in jets, in all thirty-six heavy bombers. He had won the Oak Leaves and had deserved them, but his refusal to know when he was beaten was what really made him stand out. His list of 'special engagements' was considerable and his operational reports read like an adventure story. If asked how many times he had been shot down, he had to think back before he could answer. He was as *au fait* with his parachute as his umbrella and, since he had survived this far, was endowed with more than his fair share of good luck.

As the pilot of a defective Me 109 once, he crashed into a wooden communications chalet on the edge of the airfield. The occupants were out at the time. The collision demolished the structure, the W/T equipment and the Me 109 was a total write-off. Eder had a few bruises to show for his experience. Apparently he did a cartwheel of joy when he was offered the opportunity to fly the Me 262. He never forgot his first take-off in a jet, nor the day which preceded it. He was drafted to Achmer, where he was looking forward to meeting up again with an old school friend, Alfred Täumer, who was already a pilot in the Kommando Nowotny. Upon his arrival, Eder was informed that Täumer had crashed fatally the day before. On the day of his first flight, he was waiting to take off behind Oberleutnant Bley's machine. He watched as Bley roared down the runway, had some kind of problem getting off the ground and crashed into an adjoining field. There was a burst of flame and that was the end of Bley.

Stabsingenieur Leitner, supervising Eder's first take-off, told him to get out of the machine. Leitner explained that he considered it very unfavourable to attempt a maiden take-off after having witnessed Bley's demise. Leitner thought it best for Eder to have an successful example to follow. Eder got back in his machine and prepared to follow Leitner's take-off.

At first all went well. Once in the air Eder noticed his left turbine billowing smoke and he realised that the machine was describing a long, curving turn which would bring him over the main hangar. He had little enough height, just enough to scrape the hangar roof. The contact knocked off a wing and the remainder of the airframe went through the roof into the hangar below. Eder took off again in another aircraft, admitting his fear that if he did not do so at once, he would never fly again. The second flight passed off without incident.

He reported that his first victory as a jet pilot was made 'by mistake'. He took off from Lechfeld, was directed by W/T to an enemy machine and enveloped himself in the condensation stream of the enemy aircraft. He released the safety catch of his weapons, glanced at his instrument panel and decided to attack. At that instant, before having fired, the Lightning was suddenly huge and near in front of him and there occurred forthwith the sickening crack of a collision. He had tangled with some part of the enemy fighter as he tried to rise above his opponent. Eder paused during his baling-out procedure when he noticed that his aircraft seemed in no difficulty. Both turbines were running, there were a few large bumps in the wing, but these seemed harmless, and in the end he landed safely at Lechfeld. The adventure joined the thick sheaf of reports in his personal file.

Quax Schnörrer and wingman Oberfähnrich Petermann were in a loose formation behind Eder's *Rotte* when they sighted the large bomber formation. Schnörrer reported:

We saw two waves of bombers, the larger with about twenty-seven machines and a smaller one with nine. Eder told me by W/T we would attack the smaller formation as there were only four of us. Then he said, 'Come on, Quax, we'll all attack together!' I followed his *Rotte*. The enemy formation was putting up a massive defensive fire yet I saw Eder get so close to the bombers' tails that I thought his intention must be to ram. A few seconds later two or three of the bombers were spinning through the depths to destruction. Eder got the first, Petermann, my wingman, and I the other one or two. We banked to disengage, then Eder called: 'We'll attack again!' We banked sharply to re-establish contact with the bombers and while doing this I noticed that both our wingmen had vanished. I closed up with Eder, covering his rear as another four-engined bomber began to disintegrate under his fire. After that we landed undamaged at our home airfield, where we also discovered our two wingmen had returned without mishap.

Nobody would have taken it amiss of Karl Schnörrer if he had had a breather after this intensive and successful burst of action. He had flown over 500 combat missions, had been shot down five times, landing by parachute each time and had old wounds to both knees. When he went swimming after the war he would demonstrate how his knees worked sideways as well as backwards when flexed. He had suffered his worst injury on 12 November 1943 when shot down from an altitude of 200 feet and hit the ground below a half-open 'chute; the result was a fractured skull, broken ribs, both knee joints broken and a broken arm. Not fully recovered, he resumed active flying until his final combat encounter on 30 March 1945.

On that last day his trio had been invited to a party at the Küps estate near Parchim. The splendid house was situated in magnificent parkland and many beautiful young ladies of the district would be attending. The morning had been quiet, no enemy aircraft alarms, the afternoon appeared likely to be the same, and what had happened in the air that night did not concern them. Karl Schnörrer and his friends shaved, showered, put a parting in their hair, took their best walking-out uniforms and highly polished shoes from their wardrobes and were in the act of admiring their reflections in the mirror when the alarm came: bombers over the Zuider Zee, target probably Hamburg.

Back into the wardrobes went the uniform jackets, to be replaced by flying blouses; the freshly pressed trousers and the polished shoes could remain – and they sprinted to the hangar. The Me 262s were towed to the runway, the men climbed up into cabin and strapped up – off! There were only three of them, but they made a good swarm – Schnörrer, Oberfeldwebel Helmut Lennartz, one of the best jet pilots, and the veteran ensign, Oberfähnrich Viktor Petermann. A few minutes later they were all in the air, and after a few curses at their misfortune, the young ladies of Küps were forgotten.

The destination was Hamburg, weather was good, and the three jets rose swiftly and smoothly. No enemy aircraft were yet in sight when, over Ludwigslust, Lennartz suddenly reported by W/T: 'Look me over, Quax, my turbine is smouldering.' Schnörrer bore away and drew back to let Lennartz fly past him and saw a thick ribbon of smoke pouring from the machine. 'Go back, Helmut,' he shouted, 'and make sure you get there safely.' He watched as the Oberfeldwebel's aircraft sheered out of the swarm and disappeared at the end of a wide turn.

Now he was alone with Petermann. Me 262 pilots were used to

being in a laughable numerical inferiority on every combat mission: it was very rare for an airfield to be able to have more than half-a-dozen jets ready to send up at any one time. In any case, Petermann was an old and reliable flyer at age twenty-nine. He was credited with sixty-four victories, plus one gunboat and fifty troop ferries in Russia on low-flying missions and had been awarded the Knight's Cross in 1944. Flak had robbed him of his left arm, and he flew with a prosthesis; he had been offered the opportunity to sit out the war in a sheltered ground job but preferred the cockpit of an Me 262 fighter.

Over Hamburg it was thicker than they had expected. Near Ludwigslust they reached their operational altitude and soon saw over the city a great swarm of four-engined B-17 bombers such as neither had ever seen before. Wave upon wave crossed the horizon, an endless procession. 'Another nice mess we've got ourselves into,' Quax muttered, but there was no alternative: they had to attack.

Almost wingtip-to-wingtip the two machines banked to get behind the first bomber formation where they ducked and weaved through long streams of tracer bullets and a hail of defensive fire. Petermann fired his rockets first and dismembered a heavy bomber. Parts of it spun away lazily and then the burning enemy aircraft tumbled into the depths. Schnörrer fired fractions of a second later into a bomber, but as he climbed above the wave he saw only traces of smoke and so could not claim the kill. He searched around and could not see Petermann. Schnörrer called to him over the W/T: 'Go home, Petermann, I'm attacking again!'

'Victor, Victor,' came the confirmation as Schnörrer made a wide turn in order to re-engage the American force. As he straightened up, he saw the enemy machine he had disabled enveloped in a thick cloud of smoke. He watched it begin its death dive, then roared into the murderous fire of the enemy tail-gunners. The whole formation was now concentrating on the single jet fighter attacking them. Schnörrer remained as nonchalant as if the rain of lead were hailstones, although he could feel the enemy fire ripping through the airframe. A turbine stopped, forcing him to break off and as he turned away he saw the gaping holes and bumps in the surfaces of the Me 262 wings. He looked down, picked out the familiar layout of Lüneburg and decided to attempt a forced landing. He still had 18,000 feet below him, so plenty of time still. His speed had fallen away, and he was now easy pickings if the American fighter escorts found him. For a while he thought he had got away with it, but then they were suddenly there. High to his rear he spotted the first points coming closer, two, three, four P-51s; they overshot him because he was flying so slowly and Schnörrer fired off a long burst without finding a mark. He realised at once that there was no use in continuing with the one turbine. He gained a little height, threw off the cabin hood, released the clasp of his straps and was sucked out of the cockpit before he could turn the machine on its back. A fraction of a second later he heard an sickening crash which drilled through his marrow and bones. After that it went quiet.

He let himself fall. Pulling the ripcord at this height would allow the Mustangs easy target-practice. He tumbled through the depths, felt how how his initial fast rate of fall slowed as he encountered wind resistance until finally he was dropping at a consistent 250 kph.

It was not the first time he had fallen in such a manner. It was almost like gliding, unimpeded pure flight which allowed one every freedom of movement. Before the war he had been a parachutist of wide renown who gave exhibitions from high towers; he knew now that as long as he remained a small bundle in the air, he was in no danger of being machine-gunned by an enemy fighter. They wouldn't be able to see him.

Falling inverted, slightly on his back with head down, he suddenly noticed how his right leg waggled uncontrollably between upper thigh and foot as if the joints and bones had gone. Now he understood the loud noise he had heard when leaving the aircraft: he had struck his leg against the jet's tailplane and injured himself seriously. He felt no pain, but was concerned, trying to hold the leg in both hands to stop the pendulum movement. In this manner he kept falling and finally tugged the ripcord of his parachute only when over a wood, as close as possible to the ground.

He fell between the trees without the canopy snagging fully, heard the silk rip above him, felt a short jerk and collapsed on the brown earth. He was unable to stand. With his pocket-knife he cut open the blood-soaked trouser leg and, severing the cable from his headphones, used it as a tourniquet to staunch the flow of blood. As a sensation of drowsiness swept over him, he took a Pervitin stimulant tablet, but it didn't seem to help. He bound the leg above the knee and, as the flow of blood stopped, attempted to treat the wound. His knife severed ribbons of flesh and peeled away dirty pieces of skin from the wound, then he cleaned it as well as he could from his first-aid pack before applying a sterile dressing. Once the job was finished tiredness overwhelmed him and he lost consciousness.

The sound of a discussion brought him to. An elderly nursing sister and some men were tending him. He learned that he had landed close to Nettelkamp near Uelzen. The men removed the remains of the parachute from the trees, folded the silk panels together and laid Schnörrer on the improvised hammock before carrying him to the nursing sister's house at Nettelkamp to await the ambulance from Uelzen. In the hospital there the doctors managed to save the leg, but as footballers say, he was left with one good leg and a swinger.

In the early hours of 4 April 1945, another great formation of enemy bombers was reported approaching. Major Rudolf Sinner, commander of III/JG7 and seven of his pilots prepared for the encounter. Before they took off, the information centre reported enemy fighters at 24,000 feet over Parchim. Immediately after receiving this report, they took off. The first seven jets circled the airfield widely to allow the formation to build while the eighth remained in visual contact and on lookout. The skies were nearly fully overcast, but the cloud layer relatively thin.

Sinner came out of the swathes of mist through a hole at about 1,200 feet and at once saw at a few hundred feet above him four aircraft with lancet-shaped wings. 'Thunderbolts!' he cursed, for he had not expected to make contact with the enemy so quickly after receiving information that they were at 24,000 feet. There was no avoiding the clash. At this low height, the Me 262s were still too slow to distance themselves from the threat and make a fresh approach. Surprised by the enemy tactic, to climb and level out into

159

horizontal flight at superior speed would take too long; the only response was to bank towards the enemy fighters in a steep ascent.

At first it appeared that this might have been successful. The Thunderbolts turned away sharply and offered Sinner the opportunity of following in a shallow dive, but scarcely had he begun this manoeuvre than he saw four Mustangs pursuing Schall's 262. His aircraft was in the same dilemma as he had just been in himself. Without firing off his rockets, which he wanted to keep in reserve for the bombers, he decided to try forcing the Mustangs away with his machine-guns, but immediately he saw above him to his right four more Mustangs about to fall on him in a dive. He succeeded in banking away below them but then came under fire from the rear. He was fenced in and no possibility remained to escape by climbing or diving, and at this height the jet didn't have the speed to outpace them. Oh shit! was his initial thought. Eight Mustangs had him in a pincer movement from just about every direction, and Sinner had no time to reflect on his position. It was not his failure – the fault lay with the controller who had warned of enemy fighters at 24,000 feet but not of those at 2,400 feet skirting the tops of the low cloud. This should have been evident from radar observation. He was alone with the enemy, but even if the rest of the group had been with him, the enemy were too many. Wherever he looked he saw Mustangs banking, wheeling and turning and he had the sensation that the only matter which remained to be resolved was which American fighter would fire the *coup de grâce*.

Sinner dived for the cloud. His machine was hit by the first burst before he reached it, but luck was with him and he sheltered in the mists. To rid himself of unnecessary weight and reduce the risk of explosion, he attempted to fire his R4M rockets. They failed to ignite. Two Mustangs had managed to cling to his tail. Why didn't they fire? Feverishly Sinner worked at the weapons panel, trying everything he could to set off the rockets. Nothing worked.

Thick smoke poured through the cockpit. The Mustangs below had opened fire as soon as they spotted the outline of the jet from below the cloud cover. Sinner saw at once that the left wing of his aircraft was aflame, and the fire set alight the cabin. Pointless to go on with it. Watching the enemy fighters close to his tail, he put his machine through a last evasive manoeuvre, threw off the cockpit canopy and jumped. His speed was 700 kph. He saw the tailplane pass him at a safe distance, but noticed straightaway that his parachute was damaged. The straps and some of the shroud lines entangled his right leg, and the pack was tugging and pulling from all directions.

'I'm done for,' he decided, convinced that the parachute canopy had separated from the harness and that he would fall head first into the depths with his undeveloped bundle. He was low and had not long to wait to see whether his assumption was correct. More by instinct than design he found the rip cord, jerked it – and the miracle happened. He was very close to the ground when the canopy deployed, a number of shroud lines dragged violently at his leg and revolved his body once or twice, but in the turbulence of the moment he hardly felt the braking jolt as the parachute blossomed.

Seconds later he landed – attached to the parachute by a thigh and his left arm – in a freshly ploughed field. At once he tried to unfasten the harness quick-release catch to prevent himself being dragged over the ground. The catch was jammed, and the canopy, bulging in the breeze, pulled him across the furrowed moist earth until it caught in a barbed wire fence. Two Mustangs, apparently the aircraft which had pursued him earlier, now made a low level machine-gun attack on the brightly coloured parachute. Shoulders hunched, Sinner crouched low for cover along a furrow. He heard the sharp tack-tack-tack of the machine-guns but they missed. Poor shooting, he told himself gleefully. As the two enemy fighters climbed away, Sinner at last manage to free the quick-release catch, got free of the canopy and shrouds flapping from the barbed wire and ran 30 metres to where the furrows were deeper. Being dragged by the parachute through the damp earth had given him an effective camouflage, and he felt fairly safe.

They decided on a fresh attack. The enemy fighters – two P-51s from 339 Fighter Group – had executed a wide circle, dived to the treetops of a nearby wood from where the two fat points between the delicate paintwork of their wings came directly for him… and the flak battery on the perimeter of the nearby Redlin airfield came alive at last to what the American aircraft were up to. Tracers hissed through the air, close to the attacking fighters which, despite the danger, lingered long enough to fire a few parting salvoes towards the flapping parachute silk. Their aim was too high. Clumps of earth and grass spurted up beyond the material, and then the fighters disappeared below the horizon at low level ducking under the cannonade of flak.

'Damned fuel,' Sinner murmured as he arose from his furrow, having only now noticed that he was in pain from burns. It was ten minutes before two operators from a radar station found him and drove the casualty to Jagdgruppe 10 at Redlin. He had serious burns to both hands and his face, as well as other injuries. He was not released from hospital until after hostilities had terminated. Ober-leutnant Schall was shot down by the four fighters pursuing him, but landed by parachute. Six days later his luck ran out when, landing at Parchim after a mission, he hit a bomb crater and his Me 262 exploded. Nine of JG7's thirty aircraft were lost on this date.

In late 1944, General der Flieger Adolf Galland and many other top fighter pilots were in direct conflict with the Luftwaffe High Command. Their anger was directed mainly at Reichsmarschall Goering who had identified the fighter arm as the cause of all his problems. When he relieved Galland of his post as fighter chief, the confrontation erupted into what is frequently called a 'mutiny'. The revolt involved demands for Galland to be reinstated, and at this point, Christmas 1944, Hitler intervened, asking Galland to form a unit of small squadron strength which would demonstrate the superiority of the Me 262 as a fighter. Thus Jagdverband 44 came into existence under Galland's command in early January 1945.

Of the veteran pilots of JV44 Galland wrote:

Nearly all of them had been on operations since the first day of the war. Hardly a single one had not been wounded at least once. Among the better known, there was not one who besides the highest awards for valour did not also carry a permanent reminder of battle. The Knight's Cross was almost an insignia of the uniform of our unit, so to speak. Now, after a long period of technical and numerical inferiority they wanted to experience again the feeling of superiority as aviators. For that purpose they were risking their lives once more…

Among 'the better known' besides Galland were the banished Oberst Lützow, the despised Mäcki Steinhoff, and the walking wounded: Barkhorn, Bob, Fährmann, Hohagen, Krupinski, Schnell, Wübke and others. Heinz Bär was among them. Operating from Lechfeld, mostly alone, he had been very successful with the Me 262, and finished the war with sixteen victories, one of the two most successful jet pilots. He had been commodore of JG Udet and eventually commanded JV44 from 26 April 1945 once Galland stepped down through injury. Twelve years later, on 28 April 1957, Bär lost his life when he crashed the harmless little *Zaunkönig* aircraft on a demonstration flight. As well as the known aces there were inexperienced pilots, practically novices, whom nobody would have thought to draft to the new unit had they not put their names forward voluntarily.

Jagdverband 44 came into being at Brandenburg-Briest on 10 January 1945. Preparations, flying-in of aircraft, re-training pilots, setting up the technical apparatus took two months. No sooner were they operational than the unit transferred on 31 March to Munich-Riem for the last murderous month of the Second World War.

Munich-Riem airbase became the target of endless strafing and bombing attacks by enemy aircraft. Perhaps they knew the quality of pilots who were going to operate from there. 'Two General-leutnants, two Obersts, one Oberstleutnant, three Majors, five in the rank of Hauptmann, eight Leutnants and about the same total of NCOs,' Galland wrote. Never before had there been a unit of squadron-size with so many fighter aces flying combat missions.

Munich-Riem went through a devastating experience of fire. The aerodrome was soon sown with bomb craters, scarcely an hour went by without Allied fighters arriving to vent their spleen on any target which took their fancy, weather permitting. When he took off in an Me 262, no pilot knew whether the runway would still be there when he got back. Yet none of the available reports ooze despair. Men jumped into slit trenches or holes in the ground when the bombs rained down, pilots together with ground crew and radar operators. Aircraft were towed away from the danger-spots during the alarm or raid and were then towed back once the all-clear sounded. They hammered day and night on repair work in the improvised hangar. Ground staff achieved the impossible for pilots who fought as though the war had just begun.

Unteroffizier Eduard Schallmoser was a small and doughty farmer's son from the Allgäu. One of the few attached to JV44 whom one could never call 'a veteran' or 'an expert'. On 4 March 1945 Schallmoser returned from a mission, reported a victory. It was noticed on checking his ammunition belts that he had not fired a single round. Hohagen asked for an explanation. 'I rammed him,' he confessed, more modest than proud. He had not fired his weapons because it had slipped his mind to release the safety catch. Even Galland had been guilty of this error in the heat of battle.

On 20 April 1945 Schallmoser flew as Galland's wingman against a formation of B-26s; Hohagen and his wingman made up the swarm of four. They attacked. Galland fired his rockets, knocked down two Marauders. The other aircraft fired and registered hits. Schallmoser roared past Galland, guns spitting fire, kept going and rammed a Marauder. Naturally he was reported missing, when the other three landed at Munich-Riem. Concern grew. The hoped-for telephone call never arrived. Another fine guy gone under the grinding wheels of death. A few hours later the telephone rang in the orderly's office. Schallmoser was calling from Kempten where his family lived. They sent a car for him. A little later he arrived, parachute over his arm like a raincoat. He had been so close to his parents' farm that he decided to drop in for coffee, he said shamefacedly.

Others were not so lucky, among them the best, such as Lützow, whom they never found.

13

Kurt Welter – The Most Successful
of the Me 262 Aces?

For decades since the war, Heinz Bär with fifteen or sixteen victories was considered the leading German jet-fighter ace. Recent analyses however have thrown up another contender with perhaps a better claim – Kurt Welter. His name appears in only a few books, and then with little more than a fleeting description. In Toliver and Constable's comprehensive work *Das waren die deutschen Jagdflieger-Asse* [These were the German Fighter Aces] Welter is credited with fifty-one victories (thirty-six at night) in the listings but no mention is made of him at all under the heading 'Jet-fighter Aces'. In Cajus Bekker's book *Angriffshöhe 4000* [Attack-height 4,000m] one finds on page 462 the brief reference: 'and (in the night-fighter arm) 10/NJG11, Oberleutnant Welter, held a place of honour by being the only night-fighter unit to be equipped with jet aircraft.' At page 472 in the same book the Personal Register observes: 'Oberltn. Kurt Welter, JG300, NJG11, more than fifty air-victories, fate unknown.' In volume 1, *Jagdflieger*, of Ernst Obermaier's pictorial work *Die Ritterkreuzträger der Luftwaffe 1939–1945* [Knight's Cross Holders of the Luftwaffe 1939–1945], Kurt Welter is listed with brief details and a photograph under the Oak Leaves holders.

Welter seems to have outlived all his family and had no close friends. The author Ernst Obermaier obtained possession of his wartime military identification book and Welter's career was pieced together by former Oberst Heiner Wittmer, chief of I Jagdkorps, Berlin-Treuenbrietzen. At the time when this present book was first published not all details were known, but already a picture was beginning to emerge of Welter from the available files and witness statements that here was one of the most extraordinary fighter aces of the Second World War.

Kurt Welter was born in Cologne on 25 February 1916. After leaving school he studied commerce and in 1934 volunteered as a private in the basic grade, *Flieger*, for a twelve-year period with the Luftwaffe. Following basic training he worked on the administration side and on 1 August 1940 was promoted sergeant for time served while at the flying school of Training Regiment 63, Marienbad. He must have had the benefit of a very thorough technical and aviation training programme for a drafting followed to the training branch, Quedlinburg Flight Training School, where he remained as a flying instructor until 9 August 1943. What appears certain is that during this period he made regular applications to fly operationally, but these were always denied by the Flying Schools' Kommando because he was an outstanding flight and fighter instructor and personnel of proven ability to fill these positions were in short supply. Those who knew him tell of a man at home in the cockpit of an aircraft as almost no other man was, a sure and certain flier who could shoot like William Tell.

When he arrived at Blind Flying School 10 near Altenburg on 10 August 1943, probably as a night-fighter instructor, he succeeded in making the jump to the *Wilde Sau*, the popular term for so-called 'bright night-hunting' operations on clear nights introduced by Major Hajo Herrmann. The role of *Wilde Sau* was to intercept the ever-growing Allied bomber fleets but they were desperately short of pilots. Now began Kurt Welter's unique path as a day- and night-fighter pilot. The extract below was written by war correspondent Helmut Pirath and appeared in the fighter crews' newspaper *Pauke, Pauke* (W/T slang for a victory):

Forty operational flights, thirty-three victories… and an interesting question! After exchanging the first few sentences with Kurt Welter, one knows that he comes from Cologne. Through his vigour and Rhinelander's open manner he brings an especial cordiality to the circle of his squadron comrades.

The extraordinary flying ability of this young officer is probably the reason that he was retained as a flying instructor until 1943 and his wish to serve at the front was not granted until last autumn (1943).

For seven long years, today's most successful single-engined night-fighter pilot taught his pupils [methods of] flying practice and safety procedures which he has now personally and convincingly put to the test in the face of the enemy. His series of successes is unique – or is it mere coincidence – when one discovers in Leutnant Welter's flight book only forty operational missions recorded and yet he wears not only the German Cross in Gold but has now been decorated (18 October 1944) with the Knight's Cross? It is no coincidence! His very first operational mission was a double success: over Hannover he shot down two four-engined bombers. His third combat mission had the same outcome. It is becoming ever clearer that his achievements were based on flying ability alone, for initially at that time he had had no combat experience. In this connection it is a very interesting question therefore whether flying ability or combat experience is the more valuable. When both are bound together and sealed with a soldier's luck, that must be the ideal solution. But here, undoubtedly, we have a special case, for within only a few weeks the number of victories exceeded the number of missions flown. After eleven missions he had shot down fourteen terror-bombers and day missions show that Leutnant Welter is master of all registers, for how else is it to be explained that in his first encounter with the enemy he knocked down two Mustangs and the next day another bird of the same feather? That two more Boeings went the same way, *summa summarum*: five aerial victories in four days!!!!?

The extraordinary achievement of this 28-year-old fighter pilot justifies my asking the brief question with which I began, and all the more so when one hears that he also heads the table of the Mosquito-hunters with six shot down and one rammed. In this case the success of this flight lieutenant and the circumstances surrounding his prowess prove that many kinds of influences, some unsuspected, can determine the path to victory. Accordingly one would do best of all in our struggle to believe not in miracles, but rather to believe in the wonderful. War Correspondent Helmut Pirath.

This report covers Welter's operational period from about October 1943 to the end of October 1944. For about three months – from 14 April to 6 July 1944 according to his service record – Welter was attached to an operational fliers' holding group but did not fly. Possibly he had been wounded in an exchange of fire or when ramming the Mosquito. Nothing more could be determined about this. The following occurred sometime at the beginning of July 1944.

One morning the orderly officer to Oberst Heiner Wittmer, I Jagdkorps, Berlin-Treuenbrietzen, announced a Leutnant Welter. Wittmer knew the name but not the person and was astonished to hear the reason for his visit: Welter wanted to fly night operations with the Me 262. Wittmer could scarcely believe his ears, and so Welter repeated his request unequivocally. Have you any idea what that would mean? Wittmer asked, more perplexed than believing. The new aircraft was giving problems enough by day, was still undergoing pre-operational trials at Lechfeld, and there would certainly be many more difficulties to be overcome before the 262 could be used as a night-fighter, if ever. Welter assured Wittmer he was serious and begged the help of the Oberst. He was convinced, he said, that it would work, and if not, well then, the Luftwaffe would be one jet and one pilot fewer and that wouldn't matter too much.

There now began a lengthy discussion. Wittmer put one question after another interspersed by the direst warnings about Welter's premature ideas. The latter ignored all objections. He had already gone over what was at stake. The principal difficulty lay in the return flight after a mission, especially in bad weather and on dark nights. There might be cases where he would get home via his parachute, but that was no different from how the day-fighters and the *Wilde Sau* night-fighters conducted affairs. What he really needed was good co-operation from the searchlight batteries over

Berlin. That was where he wanted to fly first of all. Primarily against Mosquitos, then the heavy bombers. Once he picked up the condensation trail of an enemy machine in the searchlight beam, that, plus the speed of the Me 262, was all he needed to close in and shoot it down. He would have to have two jets with ground crew and full powers to discuss tactical questions with the Flakführer Berlin and satellite centres and so on. He was thinking particularly of Briest, Parchim, Oranienburg and Burg near Magdeburg.

Wittmer liked the concept but was not yet persuaded. The lieutenant with the German Cross in Gold impressed him, less by his idea than the manner in which he presented it, free of any suggestion of arrogance, swank or readiness to prove one's loyalty to the cause by some act of 'fanatical self-sacrifice'. What was being advocated sounded reasonable, but Wittmer knew that it was out of the ordinary.

'And why do you want to run this risk?' he asked.

'Because I was a flying instructor for seven years and after my operational experience flying Me 109s and Fw 190s I believe I can have greater success with the 262.' There was no hint of presumption in this response.

'And you want to be a lone flier?' Wittmer gave him a long stare. 'You know what that means, I suppose?'

'I have considered it, Herr Oberst,' Welter replied without hesitation, 'At night everybody is more or less alone. No one can help another. But if I am successful, I can pass on my experiences with the 262 to other pilots and then build a small unit to see how we can progress from there. But initially I have to do it alone.'

Wittmer made his last objection: 'You have been unusually successful in your short operational career, Welter, but what if you crash in your 262? You wouldn't be the first.'

'Then I would have to say that until that point I had been lucky, Herr Oberst.'

Although Wittmer had expected this answer, it still impressed him. 'Then until now I have been lucky' struck a chord in his subconscious and at this moment he decided to help Welter as far as he could. That was easier said than done, for Wittmer had neither

the aircraft to give him, nor the ability to supply the other require-
ments, including plenipotentiary power over the flak chief of
Berlin. There were only channels, and these led to his own superior,
Beppo Schmidt, Commanding General I Jagdkorps.

In Wittmer's presence, Schmidt heard out Welter's application
and then telephoned Generaloberst Stumpff, who commanded
Luftflotte Reich.

If Welter had been a distinguished figure in his career until now,
what happened next was unique in the annals of the Luftwaffe.
Stumpff had been impressed by the fighting spirit and novel idea of
the junior ranking pilot, but even he had no power to conjure up
two aircraft – and particularly not Me 262 jets. Only Hitler could do
that. But 'channels' to Hitler went first through Goering. Oberst
von Brauchitsch was Senior ADC to Goering, and shortly he rang
Stumpff with the news that Goering was so taken by Welter's
suggestion – there is no other explanation for it – that he wished
Welter to present himself before the Reichsmarschall next morning
to discuss his plan.

After hearing Welter, even Goering was so enthusiastic that he
declared himself ready to help in whatever way he could, but there
was a serious difficulty. Because of the recent altercations between
high-level Luftwaffe chiefs respecting the Me 262, Goering felt
unable to give the order himself since Hitler was utterly out of
humour in the matter of the jet fighter. What he could suggest, on
the other hand however, was that Welter might well be able to sway
Hitler to his way of thinking.

Goering was not disappointed. Welter was summoned to make
his case to Hitler and received permission to go ahead with his
intentions. A Führer-edict to the various centres gave Welter a free
hand, two Me 262 fighters and a pool of ground crew.

From this time onwards, Kurt Welter flew only the Me 262. The
date of his first engagement flying the jet is not known, but it was
certainly earlier than March 1945, the date entered in his service
record. Both General Kammhuber and Oberst Wittmer remember
distinctly that Welter's first successes as a jet pilot were in late 1944,
and Wittmer particularly had a keen interest in how Welter's idea
worked in practice. It seems fairly well established by recent

analysis that the first date of operations was 12 December 1944. Since Hitler had given Welter plenipotentiary powers to make decisions, it is possible that the first combat missions with the jet overlapped the last he made with the Me 109. Wittmer considers this possible after he became Welter's direct superior in the autumn of 1944 when appointed commanding officer of I Jagddivision. A close co-operation developed between the two men, and Wittmer would often intervene to ensure Welter got his way in cases where the latter ran up against opposition despite the Führer-edict.

After his jet conversion training at Lechfeld, Welter looked for a suitable paved airstrip for his night operations with the Me 262 and chose Burg near Magdeburg. With his small ground team he equipped his two jets with the SN-Lichtenstein radar, the W/T 350 set and EBL–3 blind-flying equipment and made his first trial flights. According to former night-fighter pilot Rudolf Schönert, Welter decided on a stretch of the Brandenburg *autobahn* for his runway. It was a novel idea and he soon ran up against time-consuming obstruction from the 'experts' at the Reich Air Ministry but finally overwhelmed them with his powers of persuasion. The advantage of operating from the public highway was that an *autobahn* was not a priority target for enemy bombers. His service record shows that Welter flew thirty-two *Wilde Sau* missions, most at night, and probably many of these were with the Me 262. Various witnesses have stated that on his first nocturnal operation with the jet fighter he shot down four Mosquitos. The strategy he worked out with the Flakführer Berlin and the searchlight batteries was proven in practice. Illuminating condensation trails of enemy aircraft – or holding them in a cone of concentrated beams – enabled him to make his attack from the darkness with almost guaranteed success.

In February 1945 Welter was given the task of forming a special Me 262 night-fighter unit using his own brand of tactics. This was squadron 10/NJG 11, although the only entry in his service record to cover the period from 2 November 1944 until his discharge from the Luftwaffe on 11 May 1945 is 'Kommando Welter'. This appears to indicate that there was no substantial change in the nature of what he was doing from early November 1944 until the war's end and confirms that he was flying the Me 262 operationally throughout that period.

Welter's ability was such that no other pilot of his special unit managed to achieve anything approaching his success flying the Me 262 by night, and that is probably the reason why he became such a shadowy figure. He just kept on flying, victory following victory. One night, his aircraft badly damaged, close to his home *autobahn*, he decided to attempt a crash-landing. The aircraft skidded into woodland and came to a stop, allowing Welter to alight without a scratch. All landings are controlled crashes, and so far as he was concerned, this was merely another of them. He was ready to take off as scheduled next evening.

It seems certain that Welter flew every night, weather permitting. He was awarded the Knight's Cross on 18 October 1944. This award was made only seven days after he received the Front-fliers' clasp in bronze for thirty operational missions. This was uncommonly rare. He was promoted to Oberleutnant on 1 December 1944 and on 26 February 1945 received the Front-flier's clasp in silver for 60 operational missions. On 11 March 1945 Oberleutnant Welter 'Staffelkapitän 10/NJG 11 (Kommando Welter) became the 769th member of the Wehrmacht to be awarded the Oak Leaves to the Knight's Cross of the Iron Cross.'

Rudolf Schönert recalled that in May 1945, Welter told him that he had obtained ten victories with the Me 262 by night, the last two shortly before the war ended, so that official acknowledgement failed to arrive in the general confusion of the time. There must have been a misunderstanding regarding the period to which Welter was referring; Welter claimed twenty-five Mosquitos and two heavy bombers by night and two Mosquitos by day flying the Me 262. Analysis appears to confirm twenty of these victories to date making Welter the highest scoring German jet-fighter pilot.

Welter was killed at a level crossing near Leck, North Frisia in March 1949 when carelessly secured logs fell from a passing railway waggon and crushed his car.

14

A Last Flight to Cherbourg

While the aerial engagements and attacks of III/JG7 and JV 44 were pressed home with ever greater resolution and bitterness, exhaustive flight testing of the Me 262 continued at Lechfeld. Dr Caroli, Head of Flight Tests, and his test pilots Karl Baur, Gerd Lindner and – since February 1945 – Ludwig Hofmann – took off whenever weather and enemy operations permitted. The tests were aimed exclusively at discovering the reason for the failure which had cost so many Me 262 pilots their lives: the uncontrollable vertical dive which developed once the aircraft's nose dropped and its velocity approached the sound barrier. The cause was, of course, known to aerodynamics theorists and engineers: simply put, close to the speed of sound the wing profile counteracted the airstream flow. It was thought that the sound barrier, where reigned airspeeds of ten times hurricane force, speeds which, at ground level, could turn the Earth into a wilderness, could not be penetrated without changing substantially aircraft design. The theory was therefore known to aeronautical scientists and engineers, but the book about the practice had yet to be written.

The test flights from Lechfeld worked at investigating the sound barrier, feeling blindly for the causes of its treachery and dangers. 'Feeling blindly' followed a fine line between life and death. The pilots climbed to between 30,000 and 36,000 feet before making a steeply inclined dive with engines full out. At about 21,000 feet the jet would reach a speed of 950 kph, at that altitude almost the speed of sound. This was confirmed by the aircraft assuming of its own accord a much steeper inclination while in the cockpit a deep, dull roar could be heard which, growing ever louder, eventually sounded like a roll of thunder of long intensity. Shortly after this phenomenon occurred, the speed of the Me 262 increased until the aircraft gave a sudden jolt and tipped to one side. The pilot had now entered a very dangerous situation, for the aircraft would have begun a plunge for the ground out of control, and he had no means of knowing when the deflected airflow over wings and tail control surfaces would be restored and the aircraft thus answer the controls again. It would sometimes happen that the jet had barely six or nine hundred feet below him when the aircraft levelled out.

It was a test which required nerves of steel. Initiated at Lechfeld for the first time, the trials continued until brought to a conclusion by the arrival of US forces at Lechfeld on 26 April 1945. For their part, the Americans confiscated all relevant files in order to continue testing in the United States. On 14 October 1947 test pilot Charles 'Chuck' Yeager became the first man through the sound barrier flying the Bell X–1.

For months the Americans had known what valuable booty awaited them at Lechfeld and for the purpose had assembled a team from their test centre at Wright Field, Ohio. To their great surprise, a round dozen Me 262 aircraft fell into their hands un-damaged. On most other airfields, especially Salzburg, nearly all available jet fighters or bombers were blown up or set on fire, but a wiser airfield commander at Lechfeld gave instructions instead to merely 'immobilise' the machines. This was done by removing instruments or individual parts to render the machine unflyable, but it was an easy matter for the Americans to have the defects remedied often by recruiting the same technicians and ground crew who had previously worked on Me 262s.

Thus Caroli and his test pilots were fetched from their beds. Hofmann had a room at Lechfeld and so it was not long before it became the classroom for a training course where German instructors showed their American pupils how the jet engines worked. One can imagine the great interest shown by the Wright Field fliers on their first encounter close-to with the aircraft which had given their own fighters and bombers such a hard time, and no wonder too, that the strict rules against fraternisation were soon overcome. Ludwig Hofmann would soon discover this for himself.

While the courses of instruction continued without a break, Baur and Hofmann were often asked to fly into Lechfeld undamaged Me 262s situated in outlying locations, and eventually about twenty jets were assembled there. Shortly after, the Wright Field team transferred to an airfield not far from the southern outskirts of Paris. The German pilots were ordered to fly the Me 262s there with their American pupils in order to continue the training programme. It was certainly a strange twist in events that so shortly after the bitter aerial fighting over the former Reich German test pilots had set up a technical school for the benefit of their American counterparts. It was a peaceful scene of international co-operation, so to speak, which helped mend a few fences.

The order came a few weeks after the capitulation that all Me 262 aircraft were to be transferred to Cherbourg for transport by the Royal Navy carrier HMS *Reaper* to the United States and ultimately the sector of the Wright Field base which had been set aside for them. Rumour had it that the German test pilots would also make the transatlantic voyage. Although it was no more than a short, half-hour hop from Paris to Cherbourg, weather conditions ensured that the whole transfer operation took a fortnight. On a June morning in 1945, Ludwig Hofmann took the controls of the last Me 262 jet to be transferred. Colonel Harold E Watson, USAAF Air Technical Intelligence, head of the Wright Field team, was particularly attached to this last aircraft because it was the only one to be fitted with the Rheinmetall BK5 50mm anti-tank gun modified for use to shoot down Allied bomber aircraft. As thick as an elephant's trunk, the barrel projected several metres from the nose of the aircraft. The 5-cm shells lay in belts in the fuselage. This version of the Me 262 had never been operational, however. The weapon tended to jam badly and the muzzle-flash dazzled the pilot.

Hofmann had flown the machine quite a number of times and he was always relieved to scramble out of the cockpit after landing it. He feared that a crash-landing could easily result in a disastrous explosion involving the belts of 5-cm ammunition and upon receiving his flying orders suggested that gun and shells should be unshipped and brought by lorry or DC-3 to Cherbourg. Watson was not keen. 'It would of course mean a great deal of complicated work, etc., etc.'

The jet turbines started without a problem, everything else appeared to be in order, Hofmann gave the OK with both thumbs, the ground crew pulled away the chocks and the last Me 262 made off down the runway.

The aircraft rose quietly to 9,000 feet where Hofmann levelled out 500 feet below the cloud and set course for Cherbourg. He overflew the western suburbs of Paris, saw beneath him to his right the ruler-straight carriageway leading from the Champs Elysées and looked forward to the evening walk there already agreed with his colleagues. He contemplated other ideas. Would it be a good thing to go to the States? His family was in the Communist Zone of Germany; what life would be like there once the final borders were settled was anybody's guess. He was resolute not to go to America without his family. And so, what does the future hold for me? was his next question. Here there could be no answer. He had been a test pilot of almost ten years, first with gliders, then four years flying Flettner helicopters. As interesting as it was dangerous! Three or four of his predecessors had not survived the latter experience. He had been scheduled to test-fly the Natter, a manned rocket-propelled projectile. Here the idea was to take off, attack a bomber swarm, aim the Natter at an enemy aircraft and then – if one were lucky – land by parachute. But the Natter was not for Hofmann. In parachute training he had suffered a severe concussion. After hospital and convalescence came the opportunity at Messerschmitt. Perhaps the last, for in a defeated Germany the aircraft industry had been destroyed and it seemed unlikely that new types would be built while he was still young enough to be a test pilot. Maybe this was his last flight for many years. He glanced at his watch. Already he was halfway to Cherbourg. Below him the landscape had changed, and was now a patchwork of green, brown and yellow rectangles edged by small rivers, here and there the blue of a lake. In the far distance he thought he could see Caen, and after that it was only a few more minutes to…

A Last Flight to Cherbourg

A violent jolt tore him from his musing, the type of blow that made the whole aircraft shudder. Almost simultaneously, there began a series of metallic knocks and thuds against the right fuselage and cockpit panels. The aircraft began to vibrate wildly, then embarked upon a steep nose dive. Despite whatever force he exerted on the controls, the machine did not respond. Another jolt, and the control stick was knocked from his grasp as if by a giant's hand. The shaking and vibrating became ever more fierce and jerked his head against the cabin glass or the head rest, while the forces in the cockpit were so strong that he lost the ability to control his hand movements. He knew it was impossible to operate the throttle lever or calmly hold the control stick and restore the aircraft to normal flight.

Through the glazed window he saw smoke and flame billowing from the upper surface of the wing and engine nacelle and noticed that holes as big as a fist had been ripped open in the plating covering the wing. Here and there sharp, fluttering bluish flames like an acetylene torch tongued out accompanied by a dark grey smoke from rips and tears in the material. In those few turbulent seconds instinct took over from fear. There were few options. Parachute out or try a crash-landing? Could the aircraft yet be saved? And who would believe him when they saw the smashed wreckage of their valuable bounty, the pilot still alive? In his mind's eye he saw Watson's head, his hard gaze, fixed accusingly on Hofmann's own.

Hofmann grasped his left wrist with his right hand, forcing it forward in a vain attempt to reach the throttle lever. He persevered, his hands knocked against the lever and finally he grasped it. It could not be moved, the shaft was bent or jammed. He fidgeted with the mechanism of the locking lever – this clicked in place alongside it when the throttle lever was put to neutral – and gashed his hand.

There was smoke in the cabin, a dark acrid thick cloud rising from below. At first in thin swathes, then becoming thicker, making his eyes water. He glanced at the altimeter but couldn't read it: the vibrations and smoke obscured the figures. The vibrations worsened the steeper the dive became. The controls were useless.

The decision was made for him. A crash-landing was out of the question. All that was left for him to do was save his own life. With an effort he unfastened the small catch holding the securing mechanism of the cockpit hood. It flew off, the smoke dispersed and in the distance Hofmann saw the roofs of two adjacent houses. He had only a few hundred feet of height. It took him a few tries before he managed to release his seat straps, grasped the control stick with both hands, put the machine into a controlled roll, and almost as it began – as though seized by a giant's fist – was plucked from the cockpit and thrown free. He felt a powerful blow against his lower thigh, then the violent airstream, and pulled at once on the parachute D-ring.

The jerk as the parachute deployed was very violent, and he had the impression that the American Irvin 'chute might have split down the middle. His arms and legs felt dislocated, and his body received a jolt as if he had been swung against a wall. Hanging from the device, he looked up. It had not deployed perfectly, the canopy had a long crosswise rip and torn ribbons of the silk dangled from the canopy edging. It was spilling air, and Hofmann knew that the descent was too rapid.

The two houses were almost directly below him. Beyond was a pall of black smoke, rising almost vertically. He was probably 150 feet from the ground.

He glanced down and noticed that his feet were bare. He assumed that as the parachute jerked open, the speed of the fall had torn his boots and socks from his feet. Then the ground came up. Instinctively he raised his legs a little, then hit.

He felt nothing. As he awoke from a probably short lapse into unconsciousness, he found two men and a woman near him. Once he had opened his eyes they tried to lift him, but he shrugged them aside and made the effort to stand himself. He managed it – barely – but once he was upright his legs refused to bear the weight and he sank back to his knees.

They carried him the hundred yards to the house and laid him on a sofa. All the while he had his teeth clenched so as not to scream aloud at the pain. The woman brought him a cognac and said something to the men which Hofmann didn't understand.

Once she had left the room, the men relieved the pilot of his shirt and trousers, moved his arms and legs cautiously, felt his chest and pelvis and murmured a few observations between themselves which Hofmann was unable to follow. Groaning all the while he submitted to it although there was no place in his body which didn't seem to hurt; he observed watchfully the efforts of the men to discover whether anything was broken. His whole body was streaked with blood and heavily bruised. The right lower trouser leg was impregnated with the paintwork of the aircraft. This meant that he must have hit the fuselage or tailplane upon ejecting.

The woman had returned with an earthenware basin and began to rub oil very carefully over Hofmann's injuries. Until now Hofmann had said nothing. He looked at the woman, intending to thank her for her care when suddenly it occurred to him the danger in which he found himself. In no manner should he reveal that he was a German. The war had been over for less than a month and there was no knowing where the knives might be out. He was horrified at the possibility that already he might have let slip a German word from his lips without having noticed it. At the same time he realised that he now owned nothing. His attaché case with the paperwork, flying orders embellished with American stamps and his jacket containing money, letters and personal ID confirming his membership of the Wright Field detachment, all had been burned in the wreck of the Me 262. He remembered his parachute, the only proof he had. He requested the two men in sign language and with a few French phrases to bring in the parachute. They returned with a bundle of torn silk, damaged lines, harness encrusted with dirt. It was a miracle that it had held together. The American Irvin parachute was tested to withstand an opening force of 650 kph. Hofmann had baled out at probably 900 kph. Despite everything, he had been lucky…

And now he wanted to get away from the farm, as quickly as possible, for soon the police would arrive to investigate the circumstances of the crashed aircraft. It was a wonder that they hadn't put in an appearance already. Hofmann tried to raise himself from the sofa, but sank back almost at once. He asked the men to help him and, unable to raise his arms, allowed himself to be borne up by them, pleading that they should take him to an American airfield. They shrugged their shoulders uncomprehendingly.

Finally they decided to bring him to a small town nearby. A horse was harnessed to a Normandy waggon with large wheels. The woman brought two blankets and a straw mattress and he was laid on it. Then they set off. Hofmann had the parachute as his pillow. First they went down a rutted farm track beside a tract of ploughed land, at the end of which lay the smoking remains of the aircraft. The spark of hope that his papers might still be intact disappeared rapidly when he saw the wreckage. They all glanced at the bizarre heap of crumpled metal and continued on their way.

The trundling cart had no suspension and the jolting was intolerable. Hofmann asked the two farmers to stop and allow him to sit beside them on the plank serving as the coachman's seat. It was little improvement, but better than being stretched out in the cart. The rutted track seemed to be composed of a series of potholes. With every yard the torture for Hofmann became worse until finally they reached a paved highway.

The silhouette of a town came into view. A church tower, to its right some high trees, their branches in full leaf, chestnut or possibly oak. To the left the remains of an old wall and a row of poplars concealed the first houses, while to the right lay a scattering of new one-family prefabs, pink or yellow painted, an incongruous contrast to the mellowed brick of the walls enclosing the town houses.

Entering the small town Ludwig Hofmann's suffering began in earnest. Soon a knot of children and adults were following the slowly rumbling tumbril. By the time it had reached the town hall in the market place the original knot had grown to an ever increasing crowd. Men wearing official headgear appeared, spoke with gesticulations to the farmer on the cart, cast dubious glances at the barefoot man who rode beside him.

Hofmann understood none of the conversation except for the demand to descend from the vehicle and go into the police station near the town hall. This he ignored, preferring instead to remain where he was, pleading to be taken to an American airbase, in such pain as to be scarcely able to hold himself upright. A good fifteen minutes passed before the impasse was broken by the appearance of a US officer, an attractive young woman at his arm, who made their way to the waggon. A French official explained to the American that the man on the waggon was claiming to be a USAAF pilot. He persisted despite the inability of the American to understand what was being said, and the mademoiselle translated while running her fingers along the crease of her elegant friend's uniform shirt. The American listened to the Frenchman's doubts with patient amusement, glancing now and again at the strange figure on the driver's seat, then asked the man where he came from.

Hofmann bent forward, almost fainted, and told the officer that he was a German who had been flying a captured aircraft to Cherbourg on behalf of the Wright Field Kommando and had crashed. He pointed to the parachute behind him, and asked the American to confirm what he had said by contacting Colonel Watson at the earliest possible moment.

The American hesitated for an instant, spoke a few words to his ladyfriend, who passed them on in French to the official, then instructed Hofmann to follow him.

Hofmann clenched his teeth as they helped him down from the waggon, asked the American to take his parachute and tried to walk. It was impossible. The French girl slipped her arm below his, told her friend to do the same and in that manner the trio passed through the mob, crossed the market place and made for a small apartment in a side street where the almost unconscious Hofmann was laid on a divan. The American telephoned to a USAAF base about 30 kilometres away. They were sceptical. They didn't believe in a German ferry pilot working for the USAAF. Nothing was known of a missing Me 262. But if they liked to send the fellow over, they would soon sort him out. In June 1945 thousands upon thousands of Germans were on the run in Europe, probably most of them had been in the SS.

The father of the French girl offered to drive Hofmann to the US air base in his gas-driven automobile, provided Hofmann paid for the gas. The man had not yet perceived how his daughter was already the beneficiary of American wealth and trinkets, obtained for the usual consideration, while he remained in poverty. Finally he drove the German pilot, by now more dead than alive, to the US unit, got his fuel and disappeared.

The duty clerks looked at the barefoot stranger in perplexity. They listened to Hofmann's story, then roared with laughter. The room filled quickly at the sound of such hilarity. They got great pleasure making the German repeat over and over that he was a test pilot responsible for training US aircrew from Wright Field to handle the Me 262. Of course, nobody believed the story, but you could always count on an SS fugitive to give you a run for your money. And they liked that. They liked to see a bit of fighting spirit. Someone wanted to throw him out on the street, another to fetch the French police and let them finish him off, but the majority were happy to see how the tale spun out.

Hofmann pointed to his torn parachute. There was his proof. Now they really laughed, for as they rightly explained, there were hundreds of such parachutes in the woods. It went on for an hour, Hofmann struggling to remain conscious, until eventually the CO appeared. With some hesitation he took the foreigner into his room and told him to repeat his story from the very beginning. With his last reserves of energy, Hofmann began his account from the arrival of American forces at Lechfeld in April 1945, two months earlier. When he concluded his account, he asked the base commander to contact Colonel Watson at Cherbourg. The commander was indecisive. Three times his hand strayed towards the telephone receiver before finally he picked it up.

'I'm telling you, I don't believe your story,' he murmured, more to himself than to Hofmann, then finally began to dial. When Watson came to the phone at the other end, the commander asked him cautiously if he was missing an aircraft, a Messerschmitt 262…? Well yes, as a matter of fact we are short of one. Why, have you found it?

At last the ice was broken. Hofmann was brought to the sick bay where a young Jewish USAAF doctor speaking fluent German gave him an examination, an injection, bound his wounds and had him put to bed. The commander came for a short visit and the young doctor remained all night by Hofmann's side. Next morning a DC-3 landed to fetch him. He was taken to an American clinic in Paris and nursed there until he was out of danger, at which time he was returned to Lechfeld at his own request. There it would be many more months before Ludwig Hofmann was completely recovered.

Tests on the Me 262 machines brought to Wright Field included a competitive fly-off against a USAAF Lockheed P-80 jet fighter. The German aircraft demonstrated its general superiority. Ludwig Hofmann's flight with the Me 262 was the last by a German pilot below European skies. Test pilots in Britain, France, the United States, Czechoslovakia and perhaps the USSR flew them for a while before they took their place in aviation museums. One is to be found near Alexander Lippisch's Me 163 in the German Museum at Munich near the He 176 and He 178 models. The former two of these four aircraft were those which – at the cost of many pilots' lives – ushered in the most successful epoch of aviation.

15

Fritz Wendel's Closing Report, 1945

On 5 June 1945, Fritz Wendel submitted a report regarding the operational use of the Me 262 between May 1944 and the war's end. It is reproduced here unabridged and without comment because Wendel, as scarcely any other expert, has the competence to recount the impossible circumstances frustrating the proper and sensible use of the aircraft.

Wendel's report supplies the unequivocal proof that from the outset, the heads of fighter command and their experienced advisers such as Galland, Gollob, Trautloft, Dahl and the rest were not mistaken in their judgement of the aircraft's correct role. What he says confirms how opportunism, wishful thinking, error and human failing all contributed to an outstanding aircraft designed for one particular purpose being converted to a 'multi-purpose' machine, a tendency apparently impossible to eradicate which dogs us to the present day. Here is the report:

Messerschmitt AG Technical External Service
5.6.1945
Report by Flugkapitän Fritz Wendel
Re: Me 262

1 About the middle of May 1944 the order came that the Me 262 was to be used only as a bomber. At the beginning of June, Major Schenk received instructions to become operational as soon as possible with a small bomber unit. At this time the Me 262 was ready for operations as a fighter. Its radius of action was only 200 km from the home aerodrome, otherwise it had to land elsewhere, but at least an operational unit was able to accrue the necessary frontline experience.

The fitting of supplementary fuel tanks was already planned and in the autumn of 1944 the first fighter wing went operational, using the aircraft with which the front trials group had assimilated its experience. It seems probable that in June 1944 when Major Schenk received his orders the conditions for fighter, but not bomber, operations had already been met.

As regards the bomber role, the following problems remained to be dealt with:

a The range of the aircraft was insufficient for bomber operations. Its base had to lie at least 100 km behind the front line because of strong enemy fighter activity.

b The undercarriage required strengthening to accommodate the heavier starting weight with a bombload.

c The same applied to the tyres.

d Once the supplementary tanks had been fitted, it was found that a problem occurred with the trim due to a shift in the centre of gravity after releasing the bombload in a shallow dive. Because two guns had been unshipped from the nose to reduce aircraft weight, the centre of gravity was initially much further aft than originally designed.

The aircraft was fitted with two supplementary 600-litre fuel tanks, situated one forward and the other aft of the pilot. As the result of various tests in flight, and because they brought the all-up weight over the 7,000 kilos limit, it was decided to limit these tanks to 400 litres each. Complicated instructions were issued for consumption. The forward supplementary fuel tank was not equipped with a fuel gauge and the supply pump was prone to breakdown. Accordingly the actual contents of the tank at take-off were never known with any accuracy so that when the bombs were dropped there was often too much fuel in this tank. The result was a serious stability problem due to the release of the bombload combined with the aircraft being nose-heavy.

e The single-seater Me 262 had no bombsight. When bombing in an inclined dive, the reflecting gunsight had to be used. The procedure had to be worked out first and then taught to pilots.

f While this task was in hand, it was found that exceeding the permitted maximum speed of 850 kph could not be avoided with the originally fitted control surfaces. Replacement material of rolled plate had to be selected, tested and prepared prior to fitting.

g No bomb-retaining mechanism was available and would require testing once delivered.

h Numerous other modifications had to be introduced for speeds above 850 kph, for the fitting of supplementary fuel tanks and equipping the aircraft with rocket boosters for starts when laden with bombs.[7]

Once all these difficulties had been overcome, Schenk's operational flight of nine aircraft transferred to Juvincourt near Rheims at the beginning of August 1944.[8]

Two of the nine crashed on take-off. Pilots had no experience of maximum weight take-offs as there had been no time for practice. A third machine made an emergency landing at Schwäbisch Hall and remained there for overhaul. A fourth put down in a meadow just short of Juvincourt. The cause here was again pilot inexperience. Shortly before this transfer a Führer-edict had been received to the effect that:

a The Me 262 must not be flown at a speed exceeding 750 kph.

b It must not be dived.

c It must not descend below 12,000 feet when over enemy territory.

Whatever the concerns about speed which influenced the making of this order they were unfounded, for shortly before the transfer up to 1,000 kph had been achieved in angled dives on tests.[9] Bomb-aiming in horizontal flight was not possible using the reflecting gunsight. Accurate bombing was out of the question and Schenk's wing therefore had no tactical successes. The unit was disbanded at the end of October 1944 by when it had taken delivery of about 25 aircraft.

The airfields used were Juvincourt and Rheine/Westphalia. In addition to the four casualties already mentioned which involved no personal injury, other losses sustained were as follows: when transferring from Juvincourt, a fifth aircraft which had been forced to fly with the undercarriage deployed was shot down by a Spitfire. The pilot escaped unharmed. The sixth and seventh aircraft failed to return to Rheine after a bombing mission over Liège. The eighth was shot down by enemy fighters, the pilot landed safely by parachute in German territory. Following fire in a turbine the ninth lost a wing and crashed. The pilot did not survive. The tenth crashed while taking off from the bomb-damaged runway at Rheine. The pilot escaped. The eleventh aircraft was shot down by enemy fighters while landing.

Schenk's flight flew more than 400 individual sorties, many pilots recording up to six missions per day. Far more sorties were abandoned without reaching the target because of adverse weather conditions. The mechanical readiness for operations was very good. No emphasis was placed on shooting down enemy aircraft on these bombing missions. When Major Schenk made an experimental attack, however, his guns failed. It transpired that weapons testing had been ignored when the aircraft were converted to the bomber role, a serious setback when the machines reverted to being fighters later.

At the end of October 1944, Schenk's operational wing was re-absorbed into I/KG51 when the latter transferred to Rheine and Schenk himself took over as Squadron commander from Oberstleutnant Meister. I/KG51 remained continuously operational until the capitulation with a muster of 40 aircraft based at Rheine and Hopsten/Westphalia, then Giebelstadt, Rheine and Hopsten again, back to Giebelstadt and finally Leipheim. Fatalities were 1%, i.e., a pilot's life expectancy was 100 missions.

When I/KG51 went operational, the Führer-edict was rescinded to the extent that targets could be pin-pointed in a shallow-angled dive. The surviving pilots of the Schenk wing who had been trained in dive-bombing obtained the best results during practice since none of the pilots who joined later had had the benefit of instruction.

Tactical targets were selected locally as appeared appropriate at the particular time. This occurred because no targets were ever allocated to I Group by Luftwaffe High Command. Whether German ground forces had no faith in the aircrew's ability to bomb anything accurately as a result of how the Schenk wing had performed and thus never bothered to request Luftwaffe assistance, or Luftwaffe High Command simply did not order it for reasons of their own, was never determined. In November 1944 II/KG51 was formed at Schwäbisch Hall but the command structure within II/Group was unsuitable material for the task and its performance suffered accordingly.

— —

2 The reasons why the Führer decided that the Me 262 was not a fighter but a bomber are not fully known. Probably they are to be found in Adolf Hitler's destructive offensive spirit.[10] Also, the advisers in his more immediate circle, in particular Oberst Christian, seem to have fed him completely false information about the machine. Oberst Christian was the man appointed to advise Adolf Hitler in Luftwaffe affairs. Christian was conspicuous by his absence from operational airfields and Luftwaffe factories. Probably he always told Adolf Hitler what he wanted to hear. I base these assumptions on the opinion of senior Luftwaffe officers who discussed the subject with Adolf Hitler (such as Oberst Steinhoff).[11]

— —

3 At the same time as Schenk's bomber operations began in the summer of 1944, individual fighter sorties were flown against reconnaissance aircraft by units of Thierfelder's Erprobungskommando (EKdo) 262 from Lechfeld in Bavaria. These flights, although few and far between and made by aircraft without supplementary tanks, were extremely successful.

   As a result Hauptmann Nowotny was ordered by the Reichs-marschall to obtain as soon as practicable with an operational wing the proof that the Me 262 was more suited for use as a fighter against large enemy bomber formations than continuing in the bomber role. The Kommando Nowotny was formed at the beginning of October 1944 and based at Achmer and Hesepe near Rheine, Westphalia. The pilots were either experienced and drawn from various single-engine fighter Groups or raw fliers direct from training school. Nearly all were thrown into operations without receiving any jet training worthy of the name at Achmer or Hesepe. There were two short duty rosters and overall the operation was never well enough prepared to have had a chance of full success. Additionally the first encounters were with very strong USAAF formations. Although the wing received thirty aircraft during the four weeks of its existence, only three or four aircraft were ever in the air at any one time. The huge numerical superiority of the enemy and the inexperience of the younger Me 262 pilots combined to produce relatively poor results, many aircraft being destroyed by enemy fighters while taking off or landing. Others made crash-landings on the basis of incorrect instructions.

   Nowotny himself had little experience with the Me 262. He had not flown recently and on the occasion of a visit by General der Jagdflieger Galland on 8 November 1944 decided to take an aircraft up. After destroying a four-engined enemy bomber he was ambushed on the approach to the home airfield by thirty enemy fighters and shot down.

   Of the wing's thirty Me 262 aircraft, only three were undamaged, and seven pilots had been killed for 22 enemy aircraft destroyed. Following Nowotny's death, Galland ordered all pilots of the wing back to Lechfeld from where they did not return to operations until having completed a basic retraining course.

   —

4   At Lechfeld, JG7 reformed as an Me 262 fighter squadron under Oberst Steinhoff. Nowotny's former wing was absorbed in III/JG7. After all pilots of III/JG7 had flown ten hours at Lechfeld, the unit was transferred to Brandenburg-Briest, at first without aircraft. It was the winter of December 1944/January 1945 and the weather conditions prevented aircraft movements over southern Germany. Transfers to northern Germany, if possible at all, were severely restricted. As a result the aircraft were not flown up but brought by rail to Brandenburg-Briest where a team from Messerschmitt Technical External Service supervised the assembly work by JG7 ground personnel and then test-flew the aircraft. This work was also hampered by the winter weather.

At the beginning of February 1945, the supply firm Hr Dr Weber relieved the Messerschmitt team. This was an error of judgement because neither their labour force nor the supervision had any expertise with this type of aircraft. Additional to this further serious delay, the following modifications had been found necessary as a result of reports from pilots at the front:

a Cabin heating, primarily to keep the cabin perspex ice-free during rapid changes in altitude.
b Strengthened gun rings and new cartridge ejection chutes.
c Adjustable control stick giving better purchase to override forces on control surfaces.

At the beginning of January 1945, Oberst Steinhoff had been relieved of command in line with general policy to reduce the average age of squadron commodores. His replacement was Hauptmann Weissenberger, commander of non-operational Group I/JG7. It was at about this time that the first aircraft came by rail for III/JG7.

In co-operation with Major Rudolf Sinner, commander III/JG7, the Group came to a good state of operational readiness. The required strength of engineer officers for the ground staff was achieved. Flight safety drill was practised using radio location equipment and to round off the whole Group exercised in formation. In mid-February III/JG7 together with the Squadron Staff flight became operational with a total of fifty jets. At this point there was a critical shortage of kerosene and few fighters besides the Me 262 were available for air-defence of the Reich. It had originally been planned that the jets would take on the enemy fighter screen leaving the bombers at the mercy of propeller-driven fighters, but these tactics were now impossible and had to be abandoned.

It was decided to ignore the fighters and attack the enemy heavy bombers from dead ahead or the rear. The head-on attack was less dangerous but was found unsuccessful on account of the fast closing speed: on the other hand, attacks from the rear proved very rewarding. The Technical External Service now learned of a new weapons system which had been tested by EKdo 25, later JG–X led by Major Christl. This was the R4M 5-cm rocket loaded in racks beneath each wing. With the help of Major Christl at Parchim, a JG7 machine was fitted with the gear and tested, after which a whole flight of III/JG7 was so equipped and the first missions flown at the end of February 1945. Victories rose appreciably and almost every jet making contact with an enemy formation managed to shoot down at least one heavy bomber. III/JG7 with a total strength of forty aircraft shot down forty-five bombers and fifteen fighters for the loss of six pilots. These fatalities were unavoidable as a rear approach brought the jet into the bomber's strongest defensive arc of fire and hits were inevitable. A number of Me 262 losses were occasioned by the fighter being in too close proximity to a bomber as it exploded or unsuccessful attempts at landing on one engine after a fire in the other.

Even if the number of victories obtained by III/JG7 were, on the whole, not very high they were very significant proportional to the number of fighters deployed and taking into account the overwhelming enemy numerical superiority. In my opinion the enemy took note of these successes, of which the continual raids subsequently by his heavy bombers on Me 262 airfields and production centres is evidence.

I/JG7 was equipped at the same time as III/JG7 and operated from Kaltenkirchen north of Hamburg. Details of how this Group performed are not available. Pilots of II/JG7, the third of the newly formed Groups, were retrained at Lechfeld but never supplied with aircraft.

5 Concurrent with JG7, the first bomber squadron to be equipped with the Me 262 for fighter use, KG54, was ordered to operate as a bad-weather fighter wing. No pilot training was provided at either the Me 262 school nor later with Training Completion Group 262 Lechfeld and pilots were more or less left to teach themselves within the squadron. KG54 had no contact with the main fighter arm and even remained subordinated to the General der Kampfflieger. The outcome was that the squadron did not become operational until very late and their successes fell well short of those achieved by JG7.

The first pilots in particular, having a bomber training, were too cautious and demanded one modification after another to increase safety even though JG7 had provided plenty of proof that victories were attainable without all these improvements. Nevertheless, for poor-weather flying they demanded and got FuG 125 radar, the more accurate gyroscopic EZ 42 gunsight while blind-flying equipment was on order.

At about the end of January 1945, KG54 commodore Oberst-leutnant von Riedesel led sixteen jets into the first operation. Weather was unfavourable, nine-tenths to fully overcast, cloud base at 2,000 feet, upper limit 13,500 feet. The machines dispersed to comb through the cloud, quickly came upon an enemy formation and attacked without regrouping. Two certain and two probable kills were claimed. German casualties were three total losses, the commodore and two flight lieutenants being killed and another three or four machines written off although their pilots escaped with light injuries or unharmed. An order was now received that this Group could operate their fighters in all weathers, but although they took delivery of no less than 145 aircraft, no further missions appear to have been flown.

---

6   On his own initiative, Oberstleutnant Bär decided to cleanse the airspace over Lechfeld of enemy aircraft so far as his role of EJG2 commander allowed. He had made it clear to his flight instructors that if they encountered enemy aircraft during training flights they were to attack. In company with his wingman Kaczmarek he had scored eighteen victories of his own as a fighter pilot. A total of thirty enemy aircraft, ranging from lone fliers to members of large formations, were shot down by his squadron.

---

7 All pilots arriving at operational stations in the latter years of the war were poorly trained. One cause of this was the shortage of fuel but the real reason was that the whole approach was wrong. An adequate training in the theory, entirely independent of the fuel situation, was lacking, and by this I mean the type of training that used to be provided in the German commercial aircraft school.

8 Pilots coming from Training Completion Groups, irrespective of whether these were fighter or bomber, needed ten hours flying the Me 262 before being made operational. Veteran pilots required a shorter training period. However, a veteran bomber pilot rarely turned into a good fighter pilot because the bomber man had had the necessary aggressive fighting spirit bred out of him. A bomber pilot was only a crew member whereas in a single-seater he was suddenly on his own and the many-sidedness of fighter operation was a burden which few were able to master. Ferry pilots underwent only the briefest conversion course, a fact made only too obvious by the large number of Me 262 aircraft which they managed to crash.

From a purely flying point of view, the Me 262 is no more difficult to handle than the Me 109. In some respects it is easier, when setting down, for example, the nose-wheel prevents the tail-up landing accident. All that is required is a longer conversion course to acquaint pilots with the novelty of jet-turbine propulsion.

The Luftwaffe lacked a theoretical induction course aimed primarily at teaching how the turbine works and covering the subject of flight difficulties such as flying with only one engine.

Modern flying machines are a fairly complicated creation. When we are dealing, as in this case, with a completely new type of aircraft altogether it is all the more essential that pilots receive an intensive introduction to the theory before their flight conversion course. The aircraft and how the engines function must be fully understood in all respects. It would easily be possible to spend a hundred hours on this. A useful number of good instructors might have been trained in co-operation with industry and a large percentage of later accidents avoided. The best proof of that is a comparison of the accident statistics between Me 262 operational fliers and our first test pilots.

In conclusion to your questions I would like to finish by mentioning the night-fighter career of Oberleutnant Welter. He was a man who approached his duty with great zeal and was given the task of forming a night-fighter wing. Within a short time his unit's successes amounted to twenty enemy aircraft shot down at night using the Me 262 single-seater version without a single one of his own machines being damaged. Unfortunately the majority of his pilots were not possessed of the same élan and Welter himself could not devise a way of conditioning pilots for successful night operations. Nevertheless they achieved successes which in reality surpassed the victories of other single-engine night-fighter units. By the close his wing had suffered few losses because he used his own performance as an example for their operational training. His unit's aircraft were no better equipped than those of JG7 and had not been adapted with blind flying equipment or the FuG 125 radar. Victories were achieved almost exclusively in the searchlight beams above Berlin.

Signed: Fritz Wendel
Augsburg 5 June 1945.

Notes

Chapter 4

1 Sources in addition to Irving: correspondence and interviews in June 1968 and 1976 with Oberst Petersen, former head of the Luftwaffe Test Centre, Rechlin; in June 1968 with Generalleutnant Vorwald, former head of the Technical Office, Ministry of Aircraft Production; and from a statement made by Professor Messerschmitt during a German television interview, channel ZDF on 17 February 1970.

Chapter 6

2 This statement seems incorrect. A two-seater bomber proto-type Me 262A-2A-02 was completed at Augsburg as mentioned by Rust and Hess, and wrecked in the bombing raid of late February 1944. Another variant, Me 262A-2äU2, was a fast bomber having a plexiglass pulpit at the nose for the bomb-aimer. A Lotfe 7H bombsight was fitted together with bomb retention and release gear. Some authorities allege a long aerial along the fuselage for detonating bombs in mid air. Works no. 110484 was delivered to Rechlin in September 1944 and flew regularly until January 1944 when it was last logged and disappeared, possibly aboard the submarine U-234. Works No 110555 succeeded it. This aircraft was crashed behind American lines by a defecting pilot at Schrock/Lahn in March 1945.

3 The implication of this remark by Hitler appears to have been overlooked by the author. This fighter bomber was so fast that *it did not need guns*. A fighter bomber without guns is a bomber pure and simple. All explanations to the contrary were a deception to conceal the real purpose of why the Me 262 was a special-purpose bomber.

Chapter 7

4 Hitler's Luftwaffe ADC Oberstleutnant von Below recorded in his memoir *At Hitler's Side* (Greenhill Books, 2001) that Hanna Reitsch numbered among Luftwaffe pilots willing to fly kamikaze operations. Hitler was opposed to suicide missions but kept a list of volunteers. Von Below would have made Goering aware of this. The fact is, the Rhine bridges were not attacked by Luftwaffe kamikazes. Bearing in mind the date 7 March 1945 it may be that the intended purpose lay elsewhere.

5 Hitler had recognised his error at the latest by 9 January 1945 when, according to Toland J *The Last Hundred Days* (New York 1966) he comforted his secretary Traudl Junge, who had returned from a brief visit to Munich and described to him the horror of the heavy air raids on the city, assuring her that the nightmare would be at its end within a few weeks, because then the new jet fighters would have won back air supremacy over the Reich.

Chapter 9

6 Under international conventions to which all Western allies were signatories, the combat aviator descending by parachute is *hors de combat* and may not be fired upon until he lands when, provided he is not in neutral territory, he is fair game. (A paratrooper is not a combat aviator.)

Chapter 15

7 An alternative idea to supplementary fuel tanks developed originally for all fighters was to tow a fuel container with wings (*Deichselschlepp*). The aircraft drew on the fuel in the tank during the initial flight phase. These towed devices were proposed for the new jet bombers from 1943 onwards, and DFS trials with an Ar 234-B2 at Neuburg/Donau at the beginning of 1945 proved the value of the system. Heinz Bär flew the Me 262 Deichselschlepp trials. The fuel container looked like a one-tonne bomb fitted with wings and a tailplane and is generally described incorrectly as a towed bomb. (See Griehl, *Luftwaffe over America*, Greenhill Books, 2004).

8   This differs from the author's account earlier where these nine aircraft were replacements for the twelve machines of 3rd Squadron/KG51 already operational from Northern France.

9   Officially, on 14 October 1947 Captain Charles E Yeager, USAAF, was the first man through the sound barrier flying the Bell X-1 but there have been claims, apparently not much disputed by the Americans, that a Luftwaffe-flown Me 262 achieved the distinction first. The statement by Kurt Wendel appears to be a non-controversial way of making the claim immediately postwar. A computer-based performance analysis carried out in 1999 at the Munich Technical University showed that the Me 262 could exceed Mach 1. The criteria involved commencing a descent with a minimum dive angle of between 40 to 70 degrees from above 30,000 feet.

10 The great mystery surrounding the Me 262 which remains to be resolved is why Hitler was so adamant that an obvious fighter aircraft was a bomber. If Major Walter Dahl IV *Sturm-gruppe*/JG3 could talk about aircraft for three hours with Hitler and be 'astonished at Hitler's exact knowledge of technical details', then Hitler knew the difference between a fighter and a bomber. Hitler decided to build the Me 262 fleet as 'Blitzbombers', a role so important for some reason that it outweighed all the advantages for the aerial protection of Germany provided by the machine as the world's fastest fighter. It was explained by former Luftwaffe Generals Galland and Peltz that the Me 262 was a fighter aircraft and useless in the

conventional bomber role. They put the whole affair in a nutshell by asserting that the Me 262 would only be useful as a bomber if required to carry a 50-kilo bomb of tremendous destructive effect capable of destroying a town, such that the bomb need not be aimed.

11 Oberstleutnant Christian is mentioned in the memoir of Oberstleutnant Engel, Hitler's Army ADC, but oddly not in the memoir of von Below, Hitler's Luftwaffe ADC. On 26 November and 28 December 1942 at Führer HQ in the presence of Jodl, Christian argued strongly against Goering's figures for a projected air drop at Stalingrad. Who gave him the figures, and who pulled the strings, remains unknown.

Selected Sources

Bekker, Cajus *Angriffshöhe 4000: ein Kriegstagebuch der Deutschen Luftwaffe*, Oldenburg: Gerhard Stalling 1964 (*The Luftwaffe War Diaries* English translation Frank Ziegler, London: Macdonald 1964)

Dahl, Walther *Rammjäger: das letzte Aufgebot*, Heusenstamm: Orion Verlag 1972

Dieriech, Wolfgang *Kampfgeschwader 51 'Edelweiss'*, Stuttgart: Motorbuch Verlag 1973 (*Kampfgeschwader 'Edelweiss'* English translation Richard Simkins, London: Allan 1975)

Ebert, Hans J *Messerschmitt-Bolkow-Blohm: 111 MBB Flugzeuge 1913–1978*, Stuttgart: Motorbuch Verlag 1979

Freeman, Roger A *The Mighty Eighth: units, men, and machines, a history of the US 8th Air Force*, London: Jane's 1986

Galland, Adolf *Die Ersten und die Letzten: die Jagdflieger im Zweiten Weltkrieg* Darmstadt: Schneekluth 1953 (*The First and the Last*, English translation Mervyn Savill, London: Methuen & Co. 1955)

Green, William *The Warplanes of the Third Reich*, London: Macdonald and Jane's 1979

Griehl, Manfred *Luftwaffe over America*, London: Greenhill Books 2004

Heiman, Grover *Jet Pioneers*, New York: Duell, Sloan and Pearce 1963

Heinkel, Ernst *Stürmisches Leben*, Preetz: Mundus Verlag 1963

(*He 1000,* English translation Mervyn Savill, London: Hutchinson 1955)

Herlin, Hans *Udet: eines Mannes Leben und die Geschichte seiner Zeit,* Hamburg: Nannen 1958

Holliday, Joe *Mosquito,* Toronto: Doubleday Canada Ltd 1970

Irving, David *Die Tragödie der deutschen Luftwaffe: aus den Akten un Erinnerungen von Feldmarchall Milch* Frankfurt/Main: Ullstein Verlag 1971 (*The Rise and Fall of the Luftwaffe: the life of Luftwaffe Marshall Milch,* English translation David Irving, London: Weidenfeld & Nicholson 1973)

Obermaier, Ernst *Die Ritterkreuzträger der Luftwaffe 1939–1945,* Mainz: Dieter Hoffmann 1966 (English edition London: G K Scott 1966

Pirath, Helmut *40 Feindflüge, 33 Absehisse*

Rust, Kenneth C and William N Hess 'The German Jets and the USAAF' in *Journal of the American Aviation Historical Society,* vol. 8, no. 3, 1963

Steinhoff, Johannes *In Letzter Stunde: Verschwörung der Jagdflieger,* Munich: Paul List Verlag 1974

Toliver, Raymond F and Trevor J Constable *Das waren die deutschen Jagdflieger-Asse,* Stuttgart (original English edition *Fighter Aces of the Luftwaffe,* Atglen PA: Schiffer Publishing 1966)

Ziegler, Mano *Raketenjäger Me 163,* Stuttgart (*Rocket fighter: the story of the Me 163* English translation Alexander Vanags, London: Macdonald, 1963)

Ziegler, Mano *Kampf um Mach 1,* Stuttgart

Archives

Alfred Krüger, Bonn

Dornier GmbH, Neuaubing

Günter Sengfelder, Altenberg

Hans-Joachim Klein, Steinkirchen

Lorenz Rasse, Linz

Messerschmitt-Bölkow-Blohm GmbH, Ottobrunn

Index

Numbers in italics refer to plates

201

Index

Index